FAITHFUL
FAMILIES

how to raise
selfless kids
in a
self-centered world

DAVE STONE

THOMAS NELSON
Since 1798

NASHVILLE   DALLAS   MEXICO CITY   RIO DE JANEIRO

Published in Nashville, Tennessee, by Thomas Nelson. Thomas Nelson is a registered trademark of Thomas Nelson, Inc.

Thomas Nelson, Inc., titles may be purchased in bulk for educational, business, fund-raising, or sales promotional use. For information, please e-mail SpecialMarkets@ThomasNelson.com.

ISBN: 978-1-4003-1873-5

Printed in China

12 13 14 15 [RRD] 5 4 3 2 1

www.thomasnelson.com

Dedication

To Mom and Dad,

Individually and collectively you have
blessed my life immeasurably.

As parents you've modeled well the qualities
taught in this book: servanthood, generosity,
forgiveness, character, prayer, encouraging
the less fortunate, and loving your enemies.
Your constant focus on others is inspiring.

Thanks for raising me by the Book.

A very grateful son,

Dave

Table of Contents

Acknowledgments

Books take on a life of their own. The name on the front cover is simply an individual representation of a slew of others who have toiled to see the project completed.

Topping my list is a very patient and prayerful wife who has put up with a distracted husband for a few months. Thanks, Beth, for the way you honor others and for being my number one encourager!

Thanks to our kids, Savannah, Sadie, Sam, and son-in-law Patrick, who have graciously allowed me to share both highlights and lowlights from their childhoods.

These chapters have been sharpened and read by a team of great parents:

Sara Burke, Tish Cordrey, Lance and Kisa Hoeltke, Shannon Bramer, Jill Turner, Carl and Lindsay Kuhl, Nicole Smith, and Mary Cummins. Your insights were invaluable.

Thanks to the dozens of parents who were kind enough to fill out surveys and allowed me to glean from their parenting habits and ideas. Penny Stokes, thank you for being a gifted teammate and coach. Thanks to Cary Meyer, Tommy Dunn, and Ben Cross for your great help throughout this project.

Thanks to the Thomas Nelson team for believing in the *Faithful Families* series. Laura Minchew, Lisa Stilwell, Jack Countryman, Jennifer Deshler, Mike Aulisio, Amy Kerr, Katie Powell, and Jordie Deshler—thanks for your ongoing encouragement and friendship.

Taking Aim

Be devoted to one another in love.

ROMANS 12:10

M att Emmons was one shot away from claiming victory in the 2004 Olympics.

It was the 50-meter three-position rifle event. He didn't even need a bull's-eye to win. He just needed to hit the target. A slam dunk. A piece of cake. An expert marksman like Emmons could do it blindfolded, with one hand tied behind his back.

His shot should have scored an 8.1, more than enough for a gold medal. But in what was described as "an extremely rare mistake in elite competition,"[1] Emmons fired at the wrong target. Standing in lane two, he fired at the target in lane three.

His score for a good shot at the wrong target? Zero. Zilch. *Nada*. Instead of a medal, Emmons ended up with an eighth-place finish and a permanent position on the list of "The Top 10 Most Embarrassing Olympic Moments."

It doesn't matter how accurate you are if you're aiming at the wrong goal.

Keeping Your Eye on the Target

No parent leaves the maternity wing with the stated goal of raising that little bundle of joy to become a self-absorbed, spoiled brat who is oblivious to the needs of others. But even well-intentioned parents can lose their focus, and when they do, it affects their aim.

It's easy to let our focus be drawn away, to get caught up in the details and stresses of life, to give up or give in. We don't *mean* to let this happen any more than Matt Emmons intentionally shot at the wrong target. It just happens when we get distracted, when we're not paying attention, when we run out of time and energy and intentionality. When too many demands clamor for our attention.

We lose sight of the mark. We hit the wrong target. And we lose a whole lot more than a gold medal and a place in sports history.

If you want to hit the right target, you have to know what you're aiming at.

That sounds pretty simple, doesn't it?

It is simple. But it's not popular. It's not the way of modern American society. It's not even the way most Christians live in the world. The target is not success or happiness or financial security or personal fulfillment. It's not adulation or appreciation or applause. It's nothing more—and nothing less—than living out the example that Jesus gave us.

The target is raising children who are others-oriented.

And I assure you that you won't hit this goal by accident.

Husband, dad, and pastor Craig Groeschel says, "If you don't want your family to turn out like every other family, then you will need to raise them differently than everyone else."[2] In other words, don't expect this to be easy. If you always do what you've always done, then you'll always get what you've always got.

Being others-oriented is about as countercultural as it gets. Self-centeredness is so prevalent in our world that we don't even recognize it anymore. We are a society of the entitled; we think we deserve whatever we have—and then some. It was true in Jesus' day, and it's still true in our own time: what matters most in this world are money, power, and self-exaltation.

How did we become such a spoiled, self-absorbed, entitled people? Well, think about it. We want the best of everything—the best house, the best car, the best job. If we can't afford it, we charge it because, after all, we deserve it.

Even if we haven't lived that way ourselves, it's all too easy to fall into the trap once we become parents. We treat our children as if they are the center of the universe. We want to give them everything we had—and more.

Before Children (BC), we all subscribed to the belief that we wouldn't call attention to the amazing feats of our offspring. But that vow goes out the window as soon as Junior smiles, rolls over, passes gas, or takes his first step. The universe screeches to a halt while two-year-old Amy spells her last name; everyone waits with unbridled anticipation to hear Jimmy burp his way through the alphabet. All eyes and ears turn to the precious, precocious offspring; friends and family take note and feign amazement.

While it's doubtful that any of these earth-shattering skills will appear on future résumés or win anyone a slot on *America's Got Talent*, she's *your* child, and therefore she's nothing short of spectacular. And spectacular, of course, deserves spectators.

Pavlov's Puppies

Remember studying Pavlov's experiments in psychology class? Ring the bell, put out the food. Ring the bell, put out the food. Doesn't take long before the dog starts salivating at the first ring of the bell whether or not the food is there. It's called conditioning.

And we condition our children. We teach our sons and daughters what to expect by the way we treat them. If they're constantly surrounded by a gushing audience, constantly told how wonderful they are, how will they learn to put others first? If everything they want magically appears on a silver platter, how are they going to learn the value of work and sharing and generosity?

No wonder American children grow up with an ego-driven worldview where everything centers around their selfish desires. No wonder your four-year-old throws tantrums, and your fourteen-year-old thinks the universe revolves around him.

Maybe your puppies are salivating because you keep ringing the bell.

A Society of Selfishness

Consider for a moment the evolution of America's most popular magazines of the past sixty years:

Time
Life
People
Us
Self
Me

Pretty revealing, isn't it?

If our kids are growing up selfish and self-centered, it's because they are merely the by-product of *us*—of you and me. They observe our priorities and adopt our values. They sense that we lack both the backbone to say no to them and the resolve to teach them to care about others. So they take advantage of our permissiveness, our indulgence. Their attitudes reflect the way they've been conditioned.

The Jesus Target

Maybe it's time we took a step back and reevaluated. Maybe it's time to look beyond the selfishness of our culture and turn our focus back to Jesus. Maybe it's time to aim at a different set of values, to take a shot at living the way Jesus lived and teaching our children the way He taught. Simply stated, to consider others' needs before our own wants and to teach our children how to be godly, generous, giving people.

What will it take to turn the tide of selfishness—both for us and for our families?

Well, it's a process. It will demand intentional teaching, frequent modeling, and a lot of time. The practice of selflessness isn't easy, and sometimes it's even painful. Certainly it's hard to change life patterns and attitudes and ways of seeing. Your children will likely bristle and protest at first, but in time you will succeed in helping them understand. And if you do, I promise you that you will reap rewards for many years to come.

It's time to let go of the poor choices and past behaviors that have gotten us into this mess and make some potentially life-changing adjustments. As parents we have difficult decisions and challenges ahead of us; we have some hard questions to answer:

- **How do we enable our kids to become others-oriented instead of consumed with getting everything they want and all the attention?**
- **How can we motivate them to set aside their video games and actually get involved in the life of a lonely neighbor or an overlooked child?**
- **How do we raise children who naturally honor others above themselves?**
- **What are some activities we could incorporate into daily life and some traditions we could establish that would help us raise selfless kids in a self-centered world?**

If being others-oriented doesn't sound quite "normal," that's because it isn't. Our carnal, sinful nature longs for praise, attention, and accolades from others. The only place people *don't* want the front row is—you guessed it—in church.

Focusing on others doesn't happen by accident. In Romans 12, Paul challenged all Christians to be distinctive in how we interact with others. We're expected to be different: to show hospitality, to honor one another, to extend radical grace, to be inclusive, to help and honor one another, to be devoted to one another, to let our light shine.

In other words, Romans 12 calls us to be transformed. It sounds countercultural—because it is. You'll be swimming against the tide. But the earlier you start that swim, the easier it becomes.

A Word of Warning

Parents, prepare yourself. You're about to embark on a radical new way of being. You're about to disrupt your parenting and break away from cultural norms. You're about to do something that goes totally against the grain of American culture. If your goal is to keep the kids happy, spoil them rotten, and teach them to look out for number one, then put this book back on the shelf and use your money to buy your kid another gadget that will quickly end up in the back of the closet.

You have to be serious about this. Dr. Richard Dobbins says, "As long as a person can tolerate being the way they are, they are not likely to change. They may admit they need to change. They may even say they want to

Teaching children to look beyond themselves is a great target to shoot for. And the earlier you begin, the better the odds you'll hit the mark.

change . . . but until the pain of remaining the same hurts more than the pain of changing, people prefer to remain the same."[3]

Dr. Dobbins is right. We don't change when we see the light; we change when we feel the heat.

Here's my question: Do you want your children to grow up to fit society's acceptable mold—into a sheltered, ego-centric existence with the focus primarily on self? If so, you won't be alone. The majority of our culture is content to raise children in a manner that caters to their whims and keeps them happy.

It's the easier way, that's for sure. But there's a downside to this approach:

- **An unhealthy focus on your child will make life more difficult for the future spouse.**
- **Habitually giving your children whatever they want is more likely to lead to selfishness rather than service.**
- **An upbringing filled with indulgences yet void of boundaries creates insecurity instead of contentment.**
- **A child-centered home weakens your marriage.**

Matt Emmons wishes he could have his final shot over again. Knowing what he knows now, his focus and aim would be much better.

A lot of parents would tell you the same thing: after the fact, when the time has passed to shape their children's values, they insist that their focus and aim would be much better if they could take another shot. But why wait until it's too late? Let's do it now, while we still have a chance to create families that are Christ-focused and others-centered.

Teaching children to look beyond themselves is a great target to shoot for. And the earlier you begin, the better the odds you'll hit the mark.

The challenges before us are clear: to take a stand against the self-absorbed, *me*-generation attitudes that hinder us from following Jesus. To teach our children to live openly and generously with others. To replace selfishness with selflessness and entitlement with encouragement.

Come, join me on this road less traveled. Together let's learn to place the spotlight on others through serving, giving, encouraging, forgiving, and accepting.

It won't be easy. But it will have an ongoing effect in the lives of our children and grandchildren. It will leave a rich legacy for those who come after us.

It might even change the world.

2

Playing Second Fiddle

Practice playing second fiddle.

ROMANS 12:10 MSG

T here I sat in the midst of the crowded theater listening to the orchestra. Not my normal Saturday night routine, I'll admit. But some of my friends felt that I needed a little culture, so there I sat, getting a healthy dose of sophistication.

Occasionally throughout the performance, the conductor would motion to a man who played the violin and have him stand. The crowd applauded wildly. When I left that night, I took with me not only my newfound "culture," but a whole bunch of questions as to what made *that guy* so special.

And let me tell you, I got an education. Turns out *that guy* was Michael Davis, the first-chair violinist, or concertmaster. Next to the conductor, he was the Mac-daddy.

Shows you how much I know.

In time, Michael and I became good friends. But that first night I just saw him as the guy who got all the applause.

It's fun to be number one.

Not so much if you're second. The great conductor Leonard Bernstein was once asked, "What is the hardest instrument to play?" To which he replied, "Second fiddle. I can always get plenty of first violinists, but to find one who plays second violin with as much enthusiasm . . . now that's a problem."[4]

I wondered if that was literally true, or just a figure of speech. So I posed the question to my talented musician friend Michael: Is it really harder to play second-chair violin in an orchestra as opposed to first-chair?

I loved his answer. "Playing the notes isn't tougher musically," Michael said, "but you're doing a lot of the work in the background while someone else is getting the glory. First violinists get the attention; that's what makes playing second violin tough."

This musical metaphor offers an apt characterization of our culture: we don't handle it well when we do the same work but someone else gets more of the glory.

Someone once said, "It's amazing what can be accomplished when no one cares who gets the credit." These words have been attributed to both the iconic UCLA basketball coach John Wooden and to NASCAR owner Robert Yates. How wonderfully ironic that we don't quite know who to give the credit to!

Whichever man said it, you and I'd do well both to live by that truth and teach it to our children. Yet this is one of the biggest challenges for us as parents: to raise kids who accept that they don't deserve first-chair treatment.

Kids whose disposition and joy are not tied to their personal opportunities, possessions, or circumstances.

Kids who go to great lengths and derive genuine joy from elevating others.

Kids who realize that their sole purpose on earth is to glorify God and honor others.

People Are More Important Than Things

Make no mistake: this transformation starts with you. If you give your smartphone more attention than you give your loved ones, don't be surprised when video games and Facebook outrank you in your child's eyes.

And don't expect society to be in your corner. Our acquisition-hungry culture equates worth with possessions and responsibilities. The more you have, the more you spend, the more you own, the more value you have in the world's eyes.

Your children will never move toward honoring others until they genuinely believe that *you* value people over things. And without this solid foundation, all of the principles and ideas in this book are nothing more than wishful thinking.

So how do you teach your kids that people are more important than things?

By believing it yourself.

By living it.

When my kids started driving, I felt prompted to assure them that they were more important than the car itself. We hope our kids know that, but a little reinforcement never hurts, especially during that first year as your teen is strangling the steering wheel with sweaty fingers. Accidents happen, and sometimes the car goes faster than we intend. So I placed in the glove compartment, clipped to the car's registration and insurance card, the following note:

If you have found this document, it means either a police officer has pulled you over, or you have been in an accident. First, I hope you are okay and that no one was hurt. But I also hope you will hear my voice saying to you, "You are more important to me than any car."

Cars can be painted and fixed. Sometimes people can't. I love you and hope you are okay. Give me a call when the cop leaves so that I will know that you are.

Love,
Dad

PS, If you were speeding, I hope you learned your lesson. Never forget the beating of your heart when you saw the flashing lights in your rearview mirror.

(At least I've *heard* people say the heart rate increases. I wouldn't know!)

Those words might sound hokey, but in that tense moment the message won't seem that way to your teenager. It will communicate that you value people above things, that you value him or her above a car.

Enough About You ... Let's Talk About Me

Years ago a popular sitcom featured the character Stephanie Vanderkellen who was a self-consumed, spoiled rich girl raised to be the center of attention. On one show she was rambling on and on about herself and then suddenly stopped and quipped, "Well, enough about me! Let's talk about you . . . What do *you* think about me?"

Pretty funny in a sitcom, but not when it plays out in your home.

Yet it's part of the human condition, this tendency to fixate on ourselves. But it's a tendency we need to work at overcoming. The Bible is pretty clear about the kind of attitudes we ought to cultivate:

- **"Deny yourself"** (Matthew 16:24)
- **"Submit to one another"** (Ephesians 5:21)
- **"Live at peace with everyone"** (Romans 12:18)
- **"Do not think more highly of yourself than you ought [to think]"** (Romans 12:3)

In a world where every kid gets a trophy for just showing up and wish fulfillment is a daily expectation, we parents have to live in a way that is contrary to our culture if we want to raise our children to be selfless and others-centered. We have to help them understand that they're not the center of the universe, that the sun doesn't rise and set on their wants and desires. Whether they're toddlers or teens, it's never too late to go back to Scripture and show your kids that valuing other people is God's idea.

Just make sure this idea is backed up by your flesh-and-blood living example.

Your children will never move toward honoring others until they genuinely believe that *you* value people over things.

Looking into People's Hearts

Our friends Brian and Karissa Sites work hard at transferring the focus from self to others. They've taught their kids, for instance, to practice looking *into* people rather than *at* people. It's a subtle distinction that can help us walk a mile in someone else's shoes. They tell their kids to have their ears open for the things that others don't say. Sometimes the missing phrases or the deafening silence actually speaks volumes.

Each week when they take a meal or a dessert to a neighborhood family, this family has their eyes open to needs. Rather than spending three days debating the issue, they simply dive in and meet the need. They might help shovel in the winter, rake in the fall, referee street ball games in the summer. Sometimes they strategically place thank-you posters for the garbage man (Keith) or the mail carrier (Debbie).

Is it any wonder that several of the Sites's neighbors have made important spiritual decisions? Such responses are a by-product of this family honoring others by looking *into* people rather than *at* them.

Meanwhile, Back at the Symphony . . .

In a symphony, just as in life, the soaring melodies and beautiful sequences go to the first violin. The audience gravitates to the musical score, pays attention, and offers accolades to the first violin. But behind the music lies the harmony of the other instruments.

"And," as Bernstein observed, "if no one plays second fiddle, we have no harmony."[5] Then there is no symphony.

The orchestra sounds better when all the musicians play their parts.

Amazing Grace

Grace is a talented runner, but because her parents have chosen to homeschool their kids, she is—according to the state's rules—unable to compete with high school cross country teams. However, the teams have allowed her to train with them. She'd be one of the district's top runners if she were allowed to run in the meets.

Since she can't provide a benefit to the team in competition, Grace concentrates on how she can help the team merely by training with them. Her parents have challenged her to help her fellow runners by encouraging them, for instance, by being someone whom other runners can pace themselves against in practice. Having Grace play this role helps the other runners improve.

And Grace is content to play second fiddle like this. Content to run in the pack rather than at the front. To provide harmony to someone else's melody.

She's learning to run the Christian race Paul talked about in 1 Corinthians 9 rather than any worldly race. And years from now Grace will be the type of person you'll want to have on your employee team at work—someone who doesn't have to be the center of attention, someone who can make everyone else better.

Stepping Down

So, what can you do to model ways to play second fiddle and place others in the limelight?

- *Serve the Server.* When you eat out, show your kids that they can help the servers by gathering up the plates to make their job easier.
- *Let the Last Be First.* Have your kids choose sides for a playground game at school or in the neighborhood in reverse order than they would normally choose. It's as simple as getting the other captain to agree ahead of

time. Everyone will be caught off guard, and several kids will be thrilled they were chosen first instead of last.

- *Encourage One Another.* The apostle Paul said, "Encourage one another and build each other up" (1 Thessalonians 5:11). Steve and Kim Wigginton have done that quite literally. Every Sunday evening they and their three daughters write notes of encouragement to whomever God places on their hearts. Those brief notes have lifted many a spirit and kept people going when they wanted to quit.

- *Watch Your Manners.* Manners are another way to show people honor. It's not so much about knowing how to set a table as much as it is about appreciating the value of another person. Listen to this definition: "Manners are rules that we try to follow that help others as well as ourselves to feel better. The goal of proper etiquette is to help make those around us feel comfortable and valued."[6] Our goal is not a robotic "Yes, ma'am" or a halfhearted, perfunctory "May I be excused?" The pivotal point is the *why* behind such behaviors.

Here is the central principle at the core of each book in the Faithful Families series: whatever you are trying to teach your kids, you must first do yourself. Don't expect your children to be others-oriented if you never show an interest in anyone other than yourself.

You may get some creative or practical ideas from these pages, but what's far more important is your authentic concern for others. Model the concept of honoring others above yourself.

When you honor others, you begin to look like Jesus.

Playing Your Part

In college I played basketball—or, rather, I *tried* to play basketball. Our team was very talented; I was not. So I didn't see a whole lot of action. In retrospect, I think the coach put me on the team so that after the games were over, the cheerleaders would have someone to hug who wasn't all sweaty!

But our team won the conference twice, and one year we finished third in the nation in our division. One reason was that the coach constantly pulled the second team aside and reminded us that the tougher we played against the first team in practice, the better they'd play come game time. Repeatedly he told us how important we were and that without us, our team wouldn't win.

And we believed it. Those of us on the second string took pride in the team's victories. Even if we were only on the court a couple of minutes in a given game, we felt as if we had played a part in the success.

Do you know why we felt that way? Because it was true.

You can take this coach's approach with your children. You can teach them the value of being on the team. Sometimes they'll be on the starting team, while in other situations they may be playing second string. But it doesn't matter because without them, the team wouldn't win. Teach your kids the value of harmony—of playing their own part, of contributing to the success of the whole without having to be in the spotlight.

If God has blessed you with more than one child, then being team-oriented begins with the sibling relationship. My wife and I were very adamant with our children from the start: if they mistreated one another, there was always a consequence. Perhaps they wouldn't be allowed to play with their friends or would lose some other privilege. Enforcing this policy is incredibly challenging, but it truly is the starting point.

Teach your children to honor one another, to share and cooperate, to encourage and cheer one another on. If we aim our kids in an others-honoring direction, that orientation can alter the course of their lives and the lives of the people they value.

Humble Harmonizing

Remember John the Baptist? He was a pretty well-known guy, in the limelight, followed by clamoring crowds. But when Jesus showed up, some of John's disciples began to drift away and follow the new leader.

John's response? "He must increase, but I must decrease" (John 3:30 KJV). It's a "more of you and less of me" attitude.

You see, there's an internal battle taking place. Our sin nature tells us we are more important than others, but God's Word teaches we're not. In line with Scripture, then, one way we honor others is by respecting them, being polite, looking out for their needs above ours.

I love the way my friend Nicole says it: "Society screams *me,* and Jesus screams *them*." Or, as Jesus said in Matthew 23:11–12, "The greatest among you will be your servant. For whoever exalts himself will be humbled, and whoever humbles himself will be exalted" (NIV).

I went to the symphony that night to get a little culture, but in the process I discovered something radically *counter*-cultural. I saw the importance of playing second fiddle. Making harmony. Standing in the shadows and giving support to the one who's in the spotlight. Finding fulfillment in humbling yourself rather than in being exalted.

More harmony. Fewer solos.

More of others. Less of me.

Shine

Don't burn out; keep yourselves fueled and aflame.

ROMANS 12:11 MSG

It was every teenage boy's dream.

Mom and Dad were going away on a trip with some friends. My brother and I would have two whole days without the parental units around!

Dad was the dean of a Christian university, so he'd arranged for us to stay in the dorm: he and Mom were guaranteed 24/7 surveillance of their offspring. Oh, don't get me wrong. We were good kids. Just prone to mischief.

Well, when my parents left, they made a tactical error. They let the other couple drive, leaving both of our family cars parked on the college campus.

My brother, who was eighteen and should have known better, handed me the keys to our family's 1969 Dodge Dart. A real chick magnet.

"You've been a decent brother," he said. "Go have fun. Take it out for a spin on campus today if you'd like."

I was fifteen without so much as a learner's permit, never mind a real license. And I was in heaven. Like a dutiful little brother, I obeyed my older sibling and took the car out—for the entire day. I'd watch for young office assistants leaving a building and say, "Hey, do you need a ride?"

"Yeah, Dave! I need to get across campus."

"Okay, I'll drive you over and then wait and give you a ride back."

My parents had raised me to be a servant, so out of the goodness of my heart, I ran a shuttle service for those beleaguered assistants for two solid days. Call it a selfless act of compassion, a Christian service project. I was, of course, careful to remind each passenger not to tell anyone. Like a true servant, I wanted my random acts of kindness to be anonymous.

Especially to my parents.

Mom and Dad returned to town, and for a couple of days everything was quiet. It seemed that our secret was safe. Then Dad came home from work and said, "Boys, I want to see you in my study right now."

We sat there while he paced. Eventually, his eyes met ours, and with passion in his voice he said, "Is there anything you boys want to tell me?"

Well, they'd been gone for nearly three days. We had done a lot of different things . . . and we weren't exactly sure what he had on us.

Early on my brother and I had adopted a philosophy for life: never confess to a *felony* if Dad only has you for a *misdemeanor*. So we replied, "No. We have nothing to declare."

Dad, being a preacher, immediately began to spout off an impromptu parable. "A certain man went on a journey with his wife. He entrusted to his older son two sets of car keys."

Oh no . . .

"While the parents were out of town, the older brother gave a set of keys to his younger brother, who didn't have his driver's license."

Then Dad said, "What should happen to these two boys?"

Dead silence.

Again—but louder this time—he asked, "What should happen to these two boys?"

Finally my Sunday school training kicked in, and I found my voice. "As surely as the Lord lives," I said, "the elder brother must die."

My father was not amused.

I tried desperately to plead my case.

"Dad, I was just being a servant, hoping to help these poor young ladies who had to walk across the campus in the Cincinnati humidity."

Nope. He wasn't buying what I was selling. Because servanthood isn't about doing whatever you want and pretending it's an act of compassion. Servanthood is about offering yourself when it doesn't benefit your own desires.

I learned my lesson the hard way. The day I turned sixteen, my dad said, "Happy birthday, Dave, but just so you know, you're not getting your license today."

Motive Matters

Richard Foster wrote, "More than any other single way, the grace of humility is worked into our lives through the discipline of service."[7]

Humility through service? Service as an act of humility? No wonder my plan backfired. Whether you are fifteen or fifty, pride and service don't mix.

The measure of greatness is not the number of servants you have; it's the number of people you serve. But *why* you do it is every bit as important as *what* you do. Motive matters. If you want to teach your kids to serve for the right reason, teach them first to adopt a Christlike attitude that places others above themselves. Raising your kids to serve is a good thing; raising them to serve out of pure and God-honoring motives is even better.

How do you recognize pure motives?

- **If you serve when no one's watching**
- **If there's no benefit for you**
- **If the one you are serving isn't appreciative, but you do it anyway**
- **If you find true joy in helping someone else**
- **If you sacrifice where you'd like to be and what you'd like to be doing in order to keep a commitment to serve**

Our world doesn't always understand a servant's heart, and the same was true in Jesus' day. As, His popularity grew, so did the popularity of His disciples. Some of them relished this limelight, and they fell into the same trap as the rest of the culture: fame made them feel that they should be served rather than serve. The disciples' position affected their disposition: it fostered pride rather than humility.

In Mark 10, Jesus sharply challenged His followers—His inner circle as well as us today—to be distinctive and different from everyone else: to seek to serve instead of to be served.

Jesus drew this stark contrast: "Whoever wants to become great among you must be your servant, and whoever wants to be first must be slave of all. For even the Son of

Man did not come to be served, but to serve, and to give his life as a ransom for many" (Mark 10:43–45 NIV).

We're called to be different. Distinctive.

An oil executive was visiting a developing country, and while he was there, his travels took him past a leper colony. He saw a missionary nurse ministering to a leper, cleaning out an infected wound. The tycoon shook his head and said to the woman, "I wouldn't do that for a million bucks."

The nurse didn't even look up. She just kept on gently swabbing the wound and said, "Neither would I. Neither would I."

Living for the Ladder

In ways both subtle and overt, our society teaches us that the most important thing in the world is to climb the ladder of success. Every day we're bombarded with television programs, advertising, Internet sites, even friends and neighbors that drum the falsehood into us: higher, faster, richer, better. We hear it so long and so often that it becomes the subliminal rhythm behind our very heartbeats, such an integral part of our lives that we barely notice it anymore.

But make no mistake: that message affects us. It teaches us that it's okay to be selfish and possessive and greedy and grasping. It reminds us to look out for number one.

The measure
of greatness
is not the
number of
servants you
have; it's
the number
of people
you serve.

It affirms our basest instincts because, after all, we're only human.

Some people will do anything to scratch and claw their way to the top. When they're at the top of the ladder, others will have to look up to them, and they can look down on others. And that can be quite exhilarating if you have nothing else to live for.

But we do.

We have purpose.

We have direction.

We have the example of Christ.

The opening line of Rick Warren's best-selling book *The Purpose-Driven Life* reads, "It's not about you."[8] Parents, if you want to raise selfless, Christlike kids, your words and actions must communicate to your children "It's not about me." But your teaching can't stop there. You must also teach your kids "It's not about them."

Paul taught, "Do nothing out of selfish ambition or vain conceit, but in humility consider others better than yourselves" (Philippians 2:3 NIV). This is the essence of Christian living. Life is not all about me. It's not about what I want or what I can acquire. Life is not about getting people to look up to me or grabbing my fifteen minutes of fame. Life is about serving. Life is about becoming like Jesus.

Planting Seeds of Service

Servanthood is, at its very essence, countercultural. It goes against the grain. It swims upstream. It's like climbing *down* the ladder when everybody else is fighting to go up.

As a parent you need to intentionally plant some seeds to get your child to consciously think of others instead of themselves. You can start early to teach your kids to pay attention to the needs of the folks around them, to look for opportunities to be kind and compassionate, to help people out.

- Explain to your toddler, "When Mommy says it's time for us to leave Ashton's house, that's when you need to say, 'Ashton, I'll help you put your toys away.'"
- Before you walk into the post office with your six-year-old son, say, "I hope you get the chance to hold the door open for someone when we are coming or going."
- On the way to school, encourage your fourth grader to find and join that kid who is sitting alone in the lunchroom.
- Take your kids to visit a children's hospital or a retirement home.
- Put your children in settings where they can pray for others.

- **Encourage your high school son or daughter to get involved in a local service project.**

Becoming others-oriented is not a matter of flipping a switch; it's a lifestyle you cultivate. So look for opportunities to remind your kids to serve others; keep that principle at the forefront of their mind.

Plant the seed. You'll see results.

Serving Siblings

Servanthood begins at home.

For most families this fact presents a big challenge. Serving at home calls for continual reminders from Mom and Dad. Point out opportunities for service. Establish for the household the expectation that everyone will treat others with compassion and respect. When your kids begin to learn how to serve their brother or sister, you are on the edge of a breakthrough. If your children learn to notice their siblings' needs and serve them, doing so for others will be a breeze (most of the time).

Lindsay, a thirty-two-year-old Maryland mother of three, told me this story:

Last summer we were at the pool in our neighborhood, and Reagan made a new friend who was

Becoming others-oriented is not a matter of flipping a switch; it's a lifestyle you cultivate.

about a year older than she was. Reagan typically played with Quint, her younger brother, at the pool, and Quint was feeling left out. He also didn't know how to swim without water wings, so he had a hard time keeping up with the girls. Obviously the tag-along, Quint was in the middle of the pool, trying to get to Reagan and her new friend Maria. He couldn't get to them; they kept swimming away from him, and he was becoming frustrated. Then Reagan, with no prompting from me, said to her friend, "Wait, wait! I want to wait for my brother. He's not a very good swimmer."

What a huge moment for this family! Reagan clearly understood that sometimes, for the sake of family or friends, you put your own plans aside or on hold. You recognize the needs of others, and you act in response.

Reagan was learning to play second fiddle. And the music sounded beautiful to her mom.

Shine Your Light

Very early on Chris and Sara Burke began challenging four-year-old Sidney and two-year-old Jackson to "shine their light." When they take their kids to preschool or a friend's house, these parents will remind them to shine their light and again explain what that phrase means.

Shining their light at school means sharing toys, being kind to everyone at playtime, respecting teachers, obeying, and having good attitudes. Sidney likes to tell her parents afterward what she did or did not do to shine her light. She might say, "I shined my light today, but there was one time I didn't, when I didn't want to share my toy with Andrew."

Shine your light. This idea can become second nature as your children grow. They can learn to ask themselves at the end of the day, "Where did I shine my light?"

When my older daughter Savannah was dating her boyfriend Patrick, she offered this little detail that told me volumes about his character: "Dad, the last five minutes of his lunch period, Patrick goes around, picks up lunch trays, and takes them back for other students."

Patrick was well loved and popular with his classmates, and soon his friends started joining in the action. The cafeteria workers were blown away and appreciative.

Servanthood can definitely be contagious.

Yet in our attention-seeking culture, we tend to see service as a demotion when it is actually a sign of strength and self-confidence. When my future son-in-law was picking up his classmates' trash, he was opening himself up for ridicule and razzing—but he did it anyway. He took the risk because being a servant was more important to him than other people's opinions of him.

And the role of self-image in servanthood is a pivotal concept for parents to grasp. If your children have a strong and healthy self-image, they'll be primed to serve others. If they are less sure of themselves, they'll be less likely to take the risk.

The Brightest Light

What does service look like? Service is shining the light instead of seeking the spotlight. In its purest form service looks an awful lot like Jesus—and not only when He offered Himself on the cross, but throughout His entire ministry. The last shall be first; the first shall be last. The least is the greatest, and the greatest is the servant of all (Matthew 19:30, 20:26–27; Mark 9:35).

Jesus demonstrated this upside-down way of thinking by showing kindness to an outcast prostitute, by reaching out and touching a leper, and by washing the feet of His disciples. In the first-century Roman world, these things just weren't done!

Understanding that fact, imagine yourself being a disciple at the Passover meal. The servant boy hasn't shown up to wash your feet, and everybody's getting a little antsy. It's a dirty job, but somebody's got to do it. *Not me*, you think. I *don't do feet*. And nobody else seems inclined to lower himself to take on such a menial task either.

So you wait. The tension mounts. Surely someone will step up and kneel down.

And Someone does. Finally.

Out of the corner of your eye you notice movement and breathe a little sigh of relief. Then you hear the sound of water filling a basin. You feel your sandals being removed and the refreshment of having your dusty feet cleaned.

At last. Somebody else is doing the dirty work.

And then you see who it is.

It's the Rabbi. The Master. The One you've committed to follow.

And He says this:

> Do you understand what I have done for you? . . . You call me "Teacher" and "Lord," and rightly so, for that is what I am. Now that I, your Lord and Teacher, have washed your feet, you also should wash one another's feet. I have set you an example that you should do as I have done for you. Very truly I tell you, no servant is greater than his master, nor is a messenger greater than the one who sent him. (John 13:12–16)

Jesus. The Footwasher. The Servant. The Example.

The One who shows us how to let our light shine on others.

Being Jesus

One summer night years ago when I was a student pastor, I taught the teens a lesson about being others-oriented. My text was John 13, Jesus washing His disciples' feet.

To make the lesson stick, I divided the students into groups and said, "For the next two hours, I want you to go out and *be Jesus* to the city of Louisville. If Jesus were here in the flesh, where would He go, what would He do, whom would He serve? We'll meet back at my apartment in two hours and share our stories."

Two hours later, they excitedly crammed into my apartment, eager to share their stories of servanthood. One group bought ice cream cones and delivered the melting treats to elderly widows. Another group visited a church elder in the hospital and prayed with him. Still others helped out at a gas station cleaning windshields.

One group went to a nursing home and sang Christmas carols to the residents. It was August, and while the elderly folks truly enjoyed it, we later learned that the song selection had left a number of the residents confused. "This is the hottest Christmas I can remember," one man said.

Oops. Sorry. . . .

Then, after all the groups had finished talking about their adventure in serving, in straggled the final group.

I said, "Greg, where have you been?"

Greg, a high school junior, said, "Well, Dave, when we left the Shively Christian parking lot, we went over to Shively Baptist."

The entire group let out a collective "Ooohh!" Shively Baptist was our archrival in church softball and basketball.

"Really?" I said. "What did you do there for over two hours?"

"We worked some at the church, and then the pastor told us about an elderly lady who needed some yard work done. They hadn't been able to get anyone from their church to do it, so we volunteered. We drove over there and mowed, raked, and trimmed."

Greg looked back at me, "As we were leaving, the woman said, 'Thank you all so much. You kids at Shively *Baptist* are always coming to my rescue!'"

Silence descended.

"Greg," I asked, "did you tell her you all were from Shively *Christian*?"

"No," he said. "I really didn't think it mattered."

And it didn't.

Jesus didn't say, "Let your light shine before others, so that they may see your good deeds and glorify your *church or your denomination*."

He said, "Let your light shine before others, that they may see your good deeds and glorify your *Father* in heaven" (Matthew 5:16, emphasis added).

The Servant Light

About the same time of year as Christmas, the Jewish tradition celebrates the Feast of Hanukkah, an eight-day remembrance of the dedication of the temple. It's also known as the Festival of Lights, and the centerpiece of the festival is the Hanukkah menorah, a nine-branched candlestick.

During the nights of Hanukkah, the center candle of the menorah remains lit, and each night another of the eight festival candles is kindled from the center candle. Prayers are offered; blessings, chanted; and songs, sung.

That center candle is called the *shamus*—the attendant or the Servant Light.

And the blessing? It begins the same way each night: "*Barukh atah Adonai, Eloheinu, melekh ha'olam.* Blessed are you, Lord, our God, Sovereign of the universe."

Barukh. "Blessed." The root of the Hebrew word is *Barakh,* "to kneel to bless; to kneel to make rich."[9]

And that is the example Jesus gives us. Just as He was, we are to be the shamus candle, the Servant Light. Kindling the lights around us. Kneeling and offering blessings to others.

The darker our world gets, the more your light is needed. Whether you carry trays, mow lawns, visit hospitals, drive office assistants, or learn lessons from teenagers who act a lot like Jesus . . .

Let your light be kindled.

Kneel to bless others.

Shine.

4

The Heart of the Matter

Honor one another above yourselves.

ROMANS 12:10

The doorbell rang, and when my father and I opened the door, a woman was standing there with her young son. She said to my dad, "Are you Sam Stone?"

My father looked down and saw his wallet in her hand. We had turned the house upside down looking for that billfold, but hadn't found it anywhere.

"You found my wallet! Where was it?"

"My husband found it on his walk to work," she replied. "He cuts through a gas station lot, and there it was."

Dad said, "I retraced my steps, and no one had turned anything in to the employees there."

She gave him a sheepish look. "My husband didn't trust them, and this is the first opportunity we've had to bring it over."

Dad was elated to get back his driver's license and credit cards. He said to the woman, "I want to give you some type of reward."

"No, no, I don't want a reward," she said. She glanced down at her son. "I just want my little boy to grow up and be honest."

And I suspect he did—because of what he saw in his parents.

What do your kids see in you? Think of it like this. You are in the construction business. You are building your children for the future. You are raising them in order to release them from your oversight. In years to come your children will be lured to cheat on the exam, lie on the expense report, or deceive their spouse. Your children will be tempted to *keep the wallet*. In both private and public settings their integrity will be tested.

How they respond will depend on how you prepare them.

Flight Plan

If an airplane takes off from Louisville, Kentucky, and the course is accidentally altered by just two degrees, thirty minutes of airtime could make the difference between landing in Dayton, Ohio, or 117 miles away in Indianapolis, Indiana. But on a four-hour flight, those same two degrees will mean the difference between arriving in Portland, Oregon, or almost a thousand miles south, in Los Angeles, California.

The slightest course change can make a huge difference over a lifetime.

If you aim your children in the right direction, it's likely they'll end up at the desired destination. But the time to get your children on course is when they are young. And they must learn from you how to stay on course and make corrections when necessary.

So, how do we give our kids the benefit of a true compass to guide their lives? We start early to establish routines and traditions that matter.

Chores

You may be wondering what possible correlation there is between helping around the house and honoring others. For starters, chores put your child on the path of a healthy work ethic. Chores also build a sense of teamwork as family members work together to influence others—even within the home. And the responsibility of doing chores builds a child's confidence.

One of the chores that Sam and Sadie shared during their teen years was unloading the dishwasher. One unloaded the top rack, and the other, the bottom. On several occasions when Sadie was out of town for a track meet, Beth noticed that Sam would just unload his half and leave the rest for Sadie's return.

In his mind, Sam did his duty to the letter of the law, but he missed an opportunity to bless his sister by doing her work as well. But with some encouragement from his mom, Sam caught the vision—and then Beth was quick to remind him that it increases the honor if you don't call your good deed to your sister's attention!

It's *human nature* to want to keep score, to get credit, to receive applause and accolades. But the *spirit nature* is different—and our spirit nature is to make us distinct from this self-centered society. So challenge your children to find joy in helping others without getting credit for it. Make a game of being a secret blessing to those around them: "Do good—and don't get caught!" Help your children understand that their chores are not a duty, but a contribution to the teamwork of the family. And the benefits extend beyond having a smoothly running home in the present.

Researchers from Toronto, Canada, and from Macquarie University in Australia, studied children from families who were given daily chores and those who were not. They drew some interesting conclusions from their investigation:

Children who performed household chores showed more compassion for their siblings and other family members than children who did not share in family responsibility. Even more interesting was the fact that not all chores are equal. The kids who did family-care chores like setting the table, feeding the cat, or bringing in firewood showed more concern for the welfare of others than children who had only self-care responsibilities, such as making their own bed and hanging up their own clothes.

Such research validates the obvious. Whenever children participate in the care of others, they grow sensitive to human need.

Include your children in the experience of serving others daily.[10]

Chores also provide a tangible transfer of responsibilities from the parent to the child, facilitating the transition from childhood to adulthood. When they share in household tasks, kids learn to grasp the concept of pulling their own weight, and—more importantly—they develop a sense of empathy toward those around them.

Contentment

At the heart of selflessness is a spirit of contentment. From a prison cell the apostle Paul wrote this: "I know what it is to be in need, and I know what it is to have plenty. I have learned the secret of being content in any and every situation" (Philippians 4:12).

What's the secret? The next verse reveals the answer: "I can do all this through him who gives me strength" (v. 13).

The "secret" to being content is having both a deep spiritual connection with Jesus and the awareness that God is at work for our good in the events of our lives. When we understand that God is faithful to provide for us and meet our needs, we begin to see those "needs" in a different light. We come to realize that we already have all that we require for a life of contentment and godly service, and this is a key lesson to pass on to your kids. If your children see you being more concerned about spiritual disciplines than earthly possessions, they too will experience greater contentment.

Expanding our horizons can help put our kids' attitudes—as well as our own—toward earthly possessions in a healthier perspective, as Tim Greener knows. A few months ago I spoke with Tim, who is superintendent of one of America's largest Christian school systems. Among its many strengths, these schools offer a missions program that gives students experiences with other cultures and lifestyles, both locally and abroad. Those mission trips and projects have opened the students' eyes: they come home with a greater recognition and appreciation of just how blessed they are.

If your children see you being more concerned about spiritual disciplines than earthly possessions, they too will experience greater contentment.

Tim knew that program had value, but he hired a spiritual formation group to assess just how effectively the school overall was influencing the students spiritually. The group conducted over three hundred interviews with all types of students, from the spiritually solid to those on the fringe of faith. And what the group discovered was a direct correlation between gratitude, as evidence of contentment, and spiritual maturity.

When the students responded to surveys or interview questions, their gratitude for their parents, school, and teachers was positive proof that they were thinking beyond themselves. Contentment and gratitude are very accurate indicators of where our kids are spiritually.

Character

Years ago when I began playing golf, I was fascinated with how far a golf ball can fly. Being young and limber at the time, my drives went pretty far—I just wasn't always certain *where* they would end up! Soon after picking up the sport, I played golf with a man named Bill, who was in his seventies. On the first tee I outdrove him by forty yards. I thought to myself, "This isn't even going to be close."

And it wasn't. Bill beat me by ten strokes!

This older gentleman could only hit the ball 150 yards, but it was always right down the middle. That day I learned an important truth every golfer eventually discovers: *direction is more important than distance.*

It's true in golf, in flying, and in life.

A lot of well-meaning moms and dads spend a great deal of time and effort molding their children's outward behavior. It's only natural: we care about what our kids do. But think about the reality that, through repetition or intimidation, almost any creature can be taught to perform on cue—children, dogs, even circus fleas. But as your children grow older and you are with them less and less, you learn the important truth every parent must eventually discover: *beliefs are more important than behavior.*

Let me explain. If you force a child to go to church just because it's the right thing to do—and if you don't spend time encouraging that child to come to a personal faith in God along the way—you can bet your last dollar that as soon as that kid is out from under your roof, she'll spend Sunday morning in bed or at brunch or curled up on the sofa with a book. A child who says or does something merely because of a parent's expectation will quit doing it the minute there's no longer any external pressure to conform. It's a short-lived parental victory if you simply teach your kids what to do, but neglect to instruct them in the why. If they don't see any reason, significance, or benefit in doing what you've taught them, they'll stop the minute they are on their own.

Motivation matters.

Consider those three hundred student interviews at the Christian school. "The kids are telling us that when they are at school they see authentic Christianity—in the teachers, faculty, and administrators," the superintendent said. "The students comment about the way the staff prays for them and how the staff does what they say they're going to do. The faculty and administration represent to them true Christianity."

I could hear the unspoken *but*, and I was pretty sure I knew what was coming next. "But the sober finding," Tim said, "is that in a lot of cases, that's not what's happening in their homes. The interviews revealed that many of their parents aren't praying with them, they're not taking them to church, and they're not being consistent in their spiritual walk."

Once again, parents, it all comes back to you. If you have a genuine faith and are a model of Christlike character, it's quite likely your kids will imitate you. Your core values will help shape your kids' beliefs, and behavior is an outgrowth of belief. In other words, who you are determines what choices you make and how you live.

Case in point: NFL quarterback Tim Tebow who is a role model for millions. He and his two older brothers are all very athletic and highly competitive. Successful sons, wouldn't you think? Kids who make their parents proud.

But their parents always stressed character over performance.

In an effort to keep them from bragging about their sports accomplishments, these young men were not allowed to bring up in conversations to people what they had achieved on the field. Their parents taught them Proverbs 27:2: "Let someone else praise you, and not your own mouth; an outsider, and not your own lips."

While they celebrated touchdowns and victories in their household, those outward actions took a backseat to inner qualities.

"We were given a dollar if someone complimented us on our character to Mom or Dad," Tim Tebow says. "We quickly became focused on those matters—such as character and humility—rather than on trying to impress someone with our exploits on or off the field."[11]

It's never too early to emphasize character. Parents would be wise to take a page out of Mr. and Mrs. Tebow's playbook. Character counts in the Tebow household. In fact, it even paid!

Sibling Success

I f you ever wonder how your kids are doing when it comes to character and contentment, observe their interaction with their brothers and sisters. Sure, they may quarrel and roughhouse, but down deep . . .

- **Do they truly care for another?**
- **Do they celebrate one another's victories?**
- **Do they have one another's back?**

One way to answer these questions is to consider how your child handles a sibling's success. My friends Mac and Aimee have five children. Scout, their thirteen-year-old daughter, is quite talented in drama. She loves to act and recently auditioned for a commercial. Her family accompanied her for the tryout.

The casting team snagged a couple of Scout's siblings and asked them to join in the fun of auditioning. Sometime later the results came in a phone call to the parents.

Aimee sat down with Scout and told her, "They want your younger brother to be in the commercial."

"That's great!" Scout exclaimed.

Concerned about her daughter's reaction, Aimee chose her next words carefully. "Unfortunately, that means they won't be using you for this one."

In spite of her disappointment, Scout smiled and said, "That's okay. I'm so glad they chose him. He'll do great."

When Mac shared that story with me, my first thought was, *What an awesome young woman. Scout was genuinely happy for her brother.*

My second thought was, *What a tribute to Mac and Aimee's parenting.* Obviously they've raised their family to be a team instead of merely a collection of individuals.

Ever notice how it's easier to mourn with those who mourn than it is to rejoice with those who rejoice? Our self-centered human nature reasons, *I look more successful when others fail.* But not Scout. She derived genuine joy from the success of others—even from the success of her younger brother. Clearly Mac and Aimee were intentional about teaching their kids to honor and support one another. And I'm guessing they didn't allow their children to get away with speaking negatively or condescendingly about one another.

Parents need to impose serious consequences when their child disrespects a parent or sibling. If children are permitted to talk negatively about the ones whom they love the most, how will they ever learn to value "the least of these" (Matthew 25:40)?

A Matter of the Heart

As I'm writing these words, I'm at a state park, enjoying the beauty looking out from the lobby of the lodge. Twenty feet away from me a seven-year-old girl has been playing checkers with her dad. As the game ended, she drew her arm back and shouted, "I won and you know it! Say it! Say I won or I'm gonna hit you in the face."

The dad just laughed and said, "You're a sore loser."

That's true. She was a sore loser . . . who perhaps deserved a sore bottom!

All kids will try this kind of attitude and talk; the issue is whether you as a parent allow it. If there is no consequence for a sharp-tongued child, then the behavior will continue. Why would you expect it to stop?

When disrespect is tolerated, godly character cannot take root. If rebellious behaviors are unchecked by Dad now, his daughter will probably have conflict with teachers, referees, and even police officers as she grows up. All for want of a little discipline.

Second-century Christian apologist and theologian Tertullian, known as the Founder of Western Theology, said: "He who lives only to benefit himself confers on the world a benefit when he dies."[12]

How much better to confer a benefit upon the world while we live!

If we as parents concentrate more on our children's character than on their accomplishments, we help them learn the value of an interior life. We give them a moral compass that will guide them when the winds of life blow them off course. We teach them the importance of motivation. We give them the resources to follow the way of Christ and to reflect the Spirit of Christ when they're on their own.

The heart of being selfless is a matter of the heart. It's about putting our focus on God and others. And it all begins on the inside.

Sure, what we do is important—how we act, how we react, how we treat people, how we give of ourselves in the service of others. But what is even more important is *why* we do it.

That little boy who came with his mom to return my dad's wallet learned that it's worth going out of your way to be honest. Tim Tebow and his brothers learned that character is more important than accomplishment.

When we honor others out of love for Christ and a desire to be like Him, we've finally come to the heart of the matter:

The heart, where God dwells.

The heart, where love is born.

The heart, where true selflessness begins.

5

Open Heart, Open Hand

*When God's people are in need,
be ready to help them.*

ROMANS 12:13 NLT

My brother and I were in our early twenties. With college barely behind us, we were gradually emerging from the financial challenges associated with the disease of *mal-tuition*. Translation: we were unemployed, in debt, looking for jobs, and entering (reluctantly) into the real world.

Around that time our godly grandmother passed away. Without consulting anyone, without offering any of my grandmother's belongings to her children, my grandfather decided to sell the farm equipment and all of my grandmother's things at a public auction to get cash so he could buy things he wanted.

The day of the auction arrived, and, heavyhearted, my mother attended. There with her brothers, she watched as furniture, farm implements, and household goods were roughly handled, coldly criticized, and callously sold to the highest bidder.

My Uncle Phil swallowed his pride and bid on his childhood red wagon: he had long ago scrawled *Philip* across its side. My mom was interested in several items, but the one she truly wanted was her mother's handmade wedding-ring quilt. My grandmother had loved that quilt, which made it all the more precious. But my mother found herself in a bidding battle against a determined antique dealer who wanted it solely to resell for a profit.

When the price went beyond my mom's spending limit, the pain was more than she could bear. She turned and left the bidding area—and the bids soared higher.

The sight of her emotional exit from that barn is forever burned into my memory, an image of the damage caused by selfishness and greed. How different the scene might have been if my great-grandparents had raised their son to share rather than hoard. My grandfather's self-centeredness and insensitivity toward even his own children led to that scene in the auction house, a heartbreaking picture of what can happen when we live to keep rather than to share.

The Root of Selfishness

Where does selfishness come from? Well, the Bible teaches that, thanks to Adam, we all have a sinful nature. In the Psalms, David described himself as "sinful at birth, sinful from the time my mother conceived me" (Psalm 51:5). Every sin we commit can be traced back to selfishness or pride.

If you don't believe it, look at your children. One of the first words out of your toddler's mouth is "Mine!" And the chorus beings: "*My* toy. *My* mommy. *My* blankie. Mine, mine, MINE!"

And not only toddlers fall prey to the magnetism of materialism. We adults aren't immune either. We want what we want when we want it, and once we've got it, we intend to keep it—and try to acquire more. We haven't truly learned that Jesus meant it when He said, "It is more blessed to give than to receive" (Acts 20:35).

We all need to change. So how can we pave the way for that metamorphosis?

Start Early

Bob and Linda have three children. When their children were little, Dad and Mom gave each of them three containers: one marked *Giving*, another labeled *Savings,* and the third marked *Spending*.

When the kids got their allowance, they were expected to divide it accordingly: 10 percent went to *Giving*, 10 percent to *Savings*, and the rest—the remaining 80 percent—to *Spending*. This habit, introduced when the kids were very young, became a discipline they have embraced in adulthood.

My own upbringing reflects a similar habit. My grandfather might have chosen the way of selfishness, but my mom imitated her mother's generous spirit and did her best to pass that trait on to my brother and me. When we were growing up, we received an allowance in exchange for doing our chores. Every week it was split down the middle—one half was to give to the Lord's work, and the other half was for us to keep or spend. As adults, neither of us continued to give half of our income to the Lord, but that early pattern sent both of us the very clear message that we could give a lot more than the minimum tithe mentioned in the Bible. We also learned that the percentage was less important than the priority: God deserves the *firstfruits* of what we receive. To this day, we continue to give to God first, trusting that the rest will be enough to meet our needs.

And Beth and I have continued to model and teach this priority. We've raised our kids to be generous in their giving, and we long ago set forth the expectation that giving to God's kingdom would exceed the tithe. We tried to teach them early on that, since God had done so much for us, out of appreciation we should want to give to Him and to others. We've taught our kids, "You can't outgive God."

As a parent you can be very deliberate in your teaching. If your child receives an allowance, you might say, "Now how much do you think you should keep, and how much do you want to share or give to someone else?"

Or "Here are ten quarters. God tells us to give back to Him at least one of the ten we've received, so we'll set that one aside first." The simple act of teaching your children to give at least 10 percent to God can have a profound impact on them. They are learning that God can do more with 90 percent than they themselves can do with 100 percent.

Start 'em young in the habits of sharing, giving, and investing in kingdom opportunities, and those patterns will stay with your kids for a lifetime.

Practical Ways for Your Family to Give

- Take your family out to eat and choose a family in the restaurant to bless anonymously by buying their meal.
- As a family, save money for a less fortunate child to go on a special outing or attend a camp that you know he or she can't afford.
- Drive through a fast-food restaurant and pay for the person behind you in line.

- When a special need arises, raise the issue at the dinner table: "I wonder how we could help" or "I wonder what we could give."
- Anonymously give a gift card to a new neighbor to welcome the family to the neighborhood.

Remember to teach your children that their motives are just as important to God as the gift they give. Jesus said, "When you give to the needy, do not let your left hand know what your right hand is doing, so that your giving may be in secret. Then your Father, who sees what is done in secret, will reward you" (Matthew 6:3–4).

This teaching is one reason we tried to keep our giving anonymous when we could. We made it a game of keeping our act a secret. The kids loved it and learned that the value of giving was to help others rather than receive praise.

When a child starts this pattern of giving early on, it's tough to stop. As pastor and writer Warren Wiersbe says, "An open heart cannot maintain a closed hand."[13]

Christmas Giving

Christmas is a great time of year to encourage generosity in your home.

Our friends Tony and Libby feared that their kids would get wrapped up in Christmas presents—what was in it for them—and distracted from the true meaning of the celebration. So they decided to do Christmas a little differently than most folks do.

When their four children were very young, Tony and Libby began the tradition of giving three Christmas gifts. (If three were good enough for Jesus, that was good enough for them!) The parents gave two of the gifts, but everyone was very involved in that special third gift.

- **In December each child would receive a gift wrapped in gold paper, a more expensive gift that reflected the gold brought to Jesus by the wise men.**
- **The second gift, wrapped in white paper, represented frankincense for purity. This personal gift was intended to encourage the children's spiritual development. It might be a CD of Christian music, a book, or a magazine subscription.**
- **The third gift, wrapped in brown paper, was totally different from the first two. At Thanksgiving, each family member drew a name and then made a gift for that person. Since myrrh was a burial spice, this was to be a gift of sacrifice—the sacrifice of time and effort. Each year the family members opened this gift last, and this gift always turned out to be the favorite. Why? Because there was so much thought and effort put into it. This gift was truly a labor of love.**

Think about your own Christmas traditions and holiday festivities. What might your family do to combat the sense of entitlement bombarding our kids?

How about some of these options?

- **Get involved in Operation Christmas Child by hosting a packing party so your kids and their friends can fill shoeboxes with gifts for children around the world.**
- **Adopt a needy family in your own town and buy them Christmas gifts.**
- **Be generous with your time and resources by inviting someone who might be alone at Christmas into your home to share in your holiday traditions.**
- **Bake Christmas goodies and have your kids take them to a nursing home to pass out during the holiday season.**
- **Volunteer to watch the children of a single mom who has little free time to go Christmas shopping. You and your family could do the wrapping for her too.**

Whatever you choose to do, make it a gift of time and love. When we give to others because of our love for God, we are twice blessed, and others see that the love of Christ is not just talk, but action.

A Legacy of Love

I was fortunate to grow up in a home where my parents modeled lavish generosity to the Lord and others in a very natural way.

For five years my dad worked at a Christian college where many employees struggled to make ends meet. Afterward he took a ministry position at a publishing company that paid him a little bit more than he had been making at the college. So during the early 1980s, knowing the pay level of their former Bible college cronies, my parents enlisted their two sons in a series of covert operations.

From time to time my parents put money in an envelope and either typed or wrote in generic block letters the name of a professor. Then, at some point in the evening after the staff had gone home and the cleaning crew had left, it was our job to slide the envelope under that person's office door. No one ever knew the gift was from my parents, and we never told. (Until now!)

But can I let you in on another secret? My parents derived incredible joy from anonymous giving. And so did Jeff and I—even though we were simply the delivery boys.

Where did such generosity originate? Well, when my dad was a little boy, his father would take him out to a frozen food locker each year on Christmas Eve. Granddad Stone was an avid hunter, and he kept his venison there.

They'd load the car with packages of meat and then drive to the homes of several widows in the community. My dad would take the packages to the front doors. As he wished them, "Merry Christmas!" and handed them the packages of food, each lady began to cry. Dad said, "Even though the weather was cold, I felt warm inside as we went from one house to the next." No wonder in adulthood my dad enjoyed giving anonymously to his former coworkers.

Several years ago our church was in a two-year building campaign. Sam was nine when it began. We asked our members to pray and commit to giving whatever they felt the Lord laid on their heart to give. On his own, Sam prayed, and he later told us that he was committing $200! He even filled out a pledge card to make it official.

Now at the time, his only income was his allowance, and that $200 represented his entire allowance for two years. No spending money. No baseball cards. No ice cream sundaes. Every week he gave every penny of his income to the church.

We didn't tell anyone the amount Sam committed—mostly for fear it would look as if we'd coerced him into giving. But about nine months into the commitment, I spoke at a father-and-son retreat in Texas, and Sam went with me. They asked if Sam would share for a few minutes about how, as a young boy, he was living for Christ. So Sam shared some thoughts and then did a Christian rap song he'd memorized. They liked the rap so much that they asked him to do it again on Sunday morning in *all* of their worship services—for about four thousand people.

The following week Sam got a check in the mail—a love offering, if you will, in gratitude for what he had shared. Any guesses on the amount? Yep. Two hundred dollars to the penny.

Nice gift for a ten-year-old. (For a minute it caused me to consider a career in rap music.) And that specific amount reminded our entire family of God's sense of humor. Clearly, and—more importantly—Sam's generosity had not gone unnoticed by the Almighty.

God knows what He's doing.

The Legacy Continues

UCLA basketball Coach John Wooden once said, "You can't live a perfect day without doing something for someone who will never be able to repay you."[14]

That's a great philosophy for us to pass on to our kids. When we live with an attitude of generosity, it can be a key aspect of our legacy and a characteristic that will show up again and again in the branches of our family tree.

Jesus said, "It's more blessed to give than to receive." So, parents, when you give, tell the stories of His faithful provision. Let your kids know how God has provided for you—and then put this truth into action. Brag on God and remind your kids that we can't outgive Him. Besides, if you hold on to things loosely, it's more likely your kids will sense that and fixate less on what they get at Christmas and birthdays—and more on what they can give.

Second Corinthians 9:7 says, "God loves a cheerful giver." The word for *cheerful* is the source of our word *hilarious*.[15] I believe we experience this kind of hilarious joy in direct proportion to how cheerfully we give. Let your kids in on the kind of joy that is experienced when, as a family, you lavishly meet the needs of others before taking care of yourself.

Here's the bottom line: if your life screams that you live in *acquisition mode,* then your children will be less apt to be in *relinquishing mode.* Our kids must learn that giving isn't some perfunctory act that we do to be seen and recognized by others. Rather, it comes from a willing and happy heart.

Meanwhile, Back at the Barn . . .

Remember my grandfather's auction? From heaven's perspective that event must have looked like a groundswell of greed. When my mom walked away from the bartering in the barn, she was dejected and emotionally distraught. The beloved quilt—so rich in

When we live
with an attitude
of generosity,
it can be a key
aspect of our
legacy and a
characteristic
that will show
up again and
again in the
branches of our
family tree.

memories of her mom—was destined to collect dust in an antique store or, at best, be purchased by someone completely oblivious to our family story.

At that moment I felt that absolutely nothing could be done to redeem this painful scene of utter selfishness.

But I was wrong.

Little did we know that inside the barn, when Mom left, the auction took a strange twist. My older brother sized up the situation and began bidding. At the time Jeff was a dirt-poor preacher, and he had absolutely no earthly interest in quilts, but he had a lot of interest in his mother's feelings.

Several minutes later the gavel came down, the auctioneer yelled, "Sold!" and they folded up Jeff's purchase. He walked out of the auction barn and over to where Mom was standing; she was completely unaware of what had transpired. Jeff handed her the quilt and said, "I love you."

They hugged. We cried.

On that day, before my very eyes, I saw the power of generosity heal some of the deep pain caused by selfishness. A son's generosity changed in a heartbeat everyone's experience of that miserable day.

But Jeff's thoughtful act didn't come out of the blue. He had been raised by a mother who chose to emulate her own mother's godly generosity rather than her father's greed. Jeff's generosity also came from a father who taught him how to slip a gift of love under an office door in the middle of the night. And, ultimately, Jeff's action was prompted by the heart of heaven itself. By the example of God's generous and sacrificial giving of another unexpected Gift, wrapped not in a quilt but in swaddling clothes and laid in a feeding trough.

Years later my brother would say, "I spent more than I had. I paid more than I should have. But I have never regretted buying that quilt."

The words of English author Elizabeth Asquith Bibesco come to mind: "Blessed are those who can give without remembering, and take without forgetting."[16]

"For God so loved the world that he *gave*..." (John 3:16, emphasis added).

Love. Sacrifice. A legacy of generosity.

We never look more like God than when we give.

6

Be Our Guest

Practice hospitality.

ROMANS 12:13

When Brad and Karrie Wyatt moved to a new state with their four young children, they began praying that their home would become the destination point for the neighborhood kids. It wasn't long before God answered that prayer. Their unfinished basement became the gathering place, the place where all the kids congregated.

Including an awkward, obnoxious, eleven-year-old named Derrick.

It became evident pretty quickly that no one had ever taught Derrick any manners. He had a habit of just hanging out . . . in the Wyatts' garage. Once they went for a walk in the neighborhood and came home to find Derrick in their house, sitting on the couch. Apparently no one in Derrick's home knew or cared where he was or what he did.

But Brad and Karrie had prayed for people to gravitate to their home, and since their prayer had been answered, they set out to take advantage of the opportunity.

They began to teach Derrick manners and people skills, to welcome and include him, despite his immature demands and lack of self-control. The Wyatts raised the bar of their expectations for him just as they would with one of their own children. They also modeled for him a genuine faith in God and a commitment to living like Jesus.

After a couple of years, Derrick's family moved a few miles away, but the whole neighborhood had gotten wind of the Wyatts' hospitality:

- **Derrick needed attention and love.**
- **The Wyatts freely gave it.**
- **People noticed.**

Why? Because in today's culture, building relationships with our neighbors isn't at the top of our priority list. The front porch swing has been replaced by the privacy fence and the electronic garage door opener. We've made it easy to avoid those who live just a stone's throw away from our own doorstep. Nobody has time for the neighbors; we all have places to go and things to do.

But press "pause" for a minute. What would happen if families played hide-and-seek *with* their neighbors instead of *from* them?

What if parents taught their kids how to welcome people, encourage others, and practice hospitality?

In such a world the Wyatts would be the norm instead of the exception.

Start 'Em Young

Children naturally want to be helpful and hospitable. Early on, their desire to please their parents and peers is evident. Watch any typical six-year-old: he begs you to let him help, dogs your steps in the kitchen or the garage, inserts himself into whatever project you're trying to finish. But children are slow and clumsy, so we impatient parents often push them aside saying, "No, no! Get out of the way. You're slowing me down. I can do it faster by myself."

Maybe so. But then we scratch our heads and wonder what happened when that little boy is fourteen and doesn't want to mow the lawn. How did our kids get so lazy and difficult?

Let's not blame the kids. It's our fault.

Yes. Us, the parents. The so-called leaders of our families. We weren't willing to invest the time in training our children in manners, habits, and expectations. We looked at the industriousness of our children and saw only an inconvenience and an interruption.

You can't expect a return on your investment if you haven't put anything in the bank.

So if you want a different result, try a different tactic. Slow down. Put your agenda aside and teach your kids how to take pride in their work and in their ability to help someone else. Start them early. Let them help cook dinner or bake cookies or change the oil in the car. Praise them for their contributions.

Never mind the mess; never mind the mistakes.

The greatest mistake is not involving your children in the process.

Hospitality in the Home

Recently my daughter Sadie had to take a trip alone—a long, ten-hour drive. A family we know lives near the halfway point of her journey, and they offered to let her stay overnight with them. Now Sadie had never met the Jobe family, but from the moment she arrived, the two girls and their parents practiced warm and generous hospitality. On the bed in "Sadie's room" were a rose, chocolates, St. Louis Cardinals cookies, and bottled water. The five- and seven-year-old daughters had

Put your agenda aside and teach your kids how to take pride in their work and in their ability to help someone else.

each drawn her a picture and written brief notes that read, "Thank you for coming to stay with us."

Fortunately, Sadie had gone to Facebook and done some reconnaissance work of her own. She arrived prepared with her own bag of goodies, complete with candy and nail polish for each of the girls and gifts for their parents.

The result? Well, Sadie can't wait to return, and the Jobes hope it will be soon because of the role model she was for their girls. And Sadie said, "Instead of just giving me a place to stay, they made it feel like home for me!"

The Jobes made my daughter's brief visit into an event. Their preparation and planning modeled for their kids how to make others feel special and honored. Although the Jobes were the ones doing us a favor, they turned the tables and put the focus on the guest instead of calling attention to their own kindness.

Now that's hospitality!

Affecting Your Neighborhood

One December evening when our girls were little, we invited all of their neighborhood girlfriends to come and eat dinner in our home. The purpose was threefold:

- **It allowed the girls a chance to dress up and feel valued and beautiful.**
- **It afforded me an opportunity to teach my son, Sam, how to treat the opposite sex.**
- **It was a creative way to get to tell the girls the Christmas story.**

The second time we did this, Sam was four and a half. He was in charge of taking the girls' coats when they came in and then helping serve dinner. Since the girls were all dressed up, Sam and I wore suits for this special occasion. At one point in the evening, I shared with all of the girls the story of God sending Baby Jesus to earth that first Christmas. I spoke of how much God valued each girl—so much that He sent His Son to earth, to them, to us.

Then Sam went around and gave a red rose to each girl. Their faces lit up. You would have thought they'd been given a thousand dollars. But on that night they received some things that last longer than money: they'd been treated with respect, valued, and shown hospitality—and that's a potent combination.

As a couple of the girls left, they remarked to me, "I've never heard that story before." In the weeks that followed, we had the opportunity to invite them to church.

Influencing Your World

Mark and Jackie Snyder went to Indonesia on a mission trip and saw firsthand the orphanages where kids slept directly on the floor. No blankets, no pillows, nothing. There was one mattress—covered with mold from the rain leaking through the roof. Food rations were meager, and few homes in the village had either electricity or running water.

The Snyders were overwhelmed that their own kids in America had so much more than these Indonesian orphans. So when they returned home, Jackie decided to have a sleepover for moms and daughters to raise awareness of the hardships faced by people who live in developing countries. The invitation stated they were only allowed to bring a towel to sleep on—just like the kids they had seen.

Before going to the Snyders' party, one of the young invited guests, an eight-year-old girl named Bradyn Frame, sent out a letter asking for money for these kids. She raised over $320 for the orphanage and shared a testimony about how God could use each of them to make a difference.

That night all the moms and daughters spread out their towels and slept on the floor. They prayed for the kids who sleep like that every single night. In the morning they ate a breakfast of nothing but white rice. The mothers and kids discussed what it would feel like to eat only rice every day and sleep on a hard floor without any bedding. The kids each chose a picture of one of the Indonesian orphans for whom they could start praying. Clearly, this sleepover was very effective in raising awareness of the plight of others and making this group of moms and daughters more appreciative of what most of us take for granted.

Sacrificing just a little of the comfort we have come to expect. Putting ourselves in another's place for a day, or an hour, or even a few minutes. Honoring those whom the world despises or ignores.

It's a Christlike way to live.

Around the Table

Years ago Darren and Amanda Walter had our family over to their home for dinner. Before we came over they had gone to the trouble of secretly finding out the favorite drink of each of our kids. As we sat down, they brought each of our kids their favorite drink—without asking!

In the middle of the table was a bowl with slips of paper folded up. Throughout the meal we took turns reaching into the bowl for a slip of paper with a handwritten question like "What's your favorite movie?" or "If you could eat a meal with a celebrity, who would you choose?"

Not only did the conversation keep the attention of our three kids, but it even captivated the curiosity of this ADHD author! The Walters went to a lot of time and trouble to get to know our family better.

Beforehand, our kids were a bit reluctant to go to a home with no other kids. Afterward they wondered when they could return! All night the Walters took hospitality to the next level. My children couldn't tell you what we ate, how the home was decorated, or the size of their home—but they'll always remember how valued they felt. That special evening spurred our family to try to turn the spotlight on our guests whenever we have people join us for a meal.

You may be tempted to dismiss the thought of opening up your home. It's too messy or your dining room is too small or the furnishings are outdated. But those factors have nothing to do with hospitality. I've received a more genuine welcome from a woman battling AIDS in a hut in Kenya than from the owner of a million-dollar estate. It doesn't matter what your house looks like, how humble or how opulent. What matters is how you treat people, how valued they feel after spending time with you.

I can hear your objections: "Come on, Dave. Aren't you overemphasizing hospitality? Aren't you making a mountain out of a mealtime?"

Well, the concept didn't originate with me. It's woven throughout the Bible. Jesus knew the importance of hospitality. When He wanted to forge a relationship with someone, He sat down to a meal with that person.

And in Luke 24 we get another interesting perspective on the subject of hospitality. After Jesus' crucifixion and His resurrection, a couple disciples are walking along the road to Emmaus. Jesus joined them and talked to them about what had happened in Jerusalem over the preceding days and what all the events meant. This long and involved spiritual conversation lasted most of the day. But the two travelers didn't know who their companion was until they sat down to dinner together. And then, Luke reported, "Jesus was recognized by them when he broke the bread" (Luke 24:35).

God becomes known to us in the breaking of the bread. And we become known to one another when we sit down together and share a meal.

It might be "just a dinner" to you. But to others around your table, it could be the moment when they recognize Jesus for the very first time.

Do Unto Others

Clearly, as a simple meal shared in Emmaus illustrates, loving and serving others doesn't have to be some elaborate undertaking. Every Monday night for the past eight years, for instance, I've watched a boy in our neighborhood roll out the trash bins for one of his neighbors. He does it with no fanfare and no expectation of reward. It's a nice gesture and a simple way for him to honor others. Service is a close cousin of selflessness.

And sometimes service is literally a matter of being a good neighbor. I'll occasionally hear my seventeen-year-old pull into the garage, but he doesn't come inside. After several minutes I'll look out the window and see Sam rebounding for the six-year-old boy next door.

Matthew 7:12 gives us a great motivation for serving others and for teaching our children to do the same: "In everything, do to others what you would have them do to you." We call it the Golden Rule, and it's one of the most valuable pieces of advice we can ever embrace. Teach it to your children; help them focus on going the extra mile with those around them. That's what Jesus did for us.

Irresistible Love and Hospitality

Columnist Cal Thomas says, "Love talked about is easily ignored, but love demonstrated is irresistible."[17]

Remember Derrick, the obnoxious little eleven-year-old without any social skills? His family did move away from the Wyatts, but evidently what he had experienced inside the Wyatts' home made a profound impact on his

It doesn't matter what your house looks like, how humble or how opulent. What matters is how you treat people, how valued they feel after spending time with you.

life. Although he lived over two miles away and had no bike or a car, he still found his way back to their home. He sought them out. Their loving acceptance was like a gravitational pull.

God continued to deepen that relationship. Brad and Karrie became the parents that Derrick never had. Brad taught him how to drive, they helped him land his first part-time job, they coached him on how to manage the small amount of money he had, and whenever there was a family member's birthday, he was included in the celebration. To this day, Derrick calls them Mom and Dad.

Different race, different house, different life experiences—and none of that matters. To him Brad and Karrie are his family.

Now seventeen, Derrick is keenly aware that his life has turned out quite differently than if he'd stayed in the direction it was heading. He just returned from a trip with his church youth group, where he made some important decisions about his life and future.

You see, while the Wyatts were pouring life lessons into Derrick, taking him to church, teaching him how to treat others, and strengthening his self-image with genuine love and acceptance, somehow during that process Derrick fell in love with Jesus Christ.

Go figure.

7

Radical Grace

*Bless those who persecute you. Don't curse
them; pray that God will bless them. . . .
Never pay back evil with more evil.*

ROMANS 12:14, 17 NLT

D ear John," the letter began.

Yep. A real-life *Dear John* letter, written to a young American soldier stationed in Afghanistan. Exhausted, scared, and thousands of miles from home, John had counted on the faithfulness of his girlfriend back home. He was devastated.

And it only got worse. At the end of the letter, his girl wrote, "Please return my favorite picture of myself, because I would like to use that photograph for my engagement picture in the county newspaper."

Ouch!

Then John's buddies came to his rescue. They rifled through the barracks collecting pictures of all their girlfriends. When they had a whole shoebox full, the jilted soldier mailed the photos to his ex-girlfriend, along with this note:

Please find your picture and return the rest. For the life of me, I can't remember which one you were.

Admit it. You're smiling. How do I know? Because human nature relishes judgment. We're programmed to prefer justice to mercy. We like things to be fair. We applaud when the ax falls, when—provided we're not the guilty party—somebody who's done wrong gets what's coming to them.

Brace yourself. You're about to be stretched out of your comfort zone.

The Grace Way

Jesus commanded, "Love your enemies, do good to those who hate you, bless those who curse you, pray for those who mistreat you" (Luke 6:27–28).

He's kidding, right?

Loving your enemies goes against the grain of reason. It's radically countercultural. Besides that, it just feels . . . wrong.

Doesn't Jesus understand how unfair life is and how cruel people can be? Doesn't He get it that blessing those who curse you is radical and revolutionary? Doesn't He know that mean people need to be put in their place?

Jesus knew. He was no stranger to human nature. But He also saw the bigger picture.

He understood the importance of *grace*.

It's a word we Christians use all the time. We depend on the grace of God for our salvation as well as for our ongoing transformation into the image of Christ. We sing, "Amazing grace, how sweet the sound . . ." And in some formal church settings, members may greet one another by saying: "Grace and peace be unto you."

But grace works both ways. We are not only to receive it; we're also called to offer it to others, to live it out on a daily basis, to extend the grace of God in the midst of difficult and trying and sometimes unfair circumstances.

We are called to be Christ in the world, to serve as God's ambassadors. And if we want to raise children who will follow in the path of Jesus, we need to model for them what it means to pray for those who mistreat us and to do good to those who despise us.

Sooner or later, no matter how much you try to protect them, your kids will come face-to-face with the reality of a broken world:

- a four-year-old bullied by a bigger child at preschool
- a nine-year-old ostracized at church because she doesn't have the right clothes
- a thirteen-year-old mocked because of his weight
- a teenage daughter victimized by lies and rumors about her purity

It's difficult enough to turn the other cheek when someone is cruel to us. But when someone belittles, betrays, or bullies our babies, it's almost more than we can stand.

Accept it. You can't fight your children's battles for them. You're one layer removed. While the circumstances may burn you up, tick you off, and make you want to strike back, the only thing you can do is pray, give wise counsel, and try to walk the painful journey with them.

Oh, and one other thing . . .

You can teach them, through your words and your example, that peace comes from the inside, from our relationship with God, and even from extending love and forgiveness to those who hurt us. In fact, extending love and forgiveness is the surest way to let our light shine.

Grace works both ways. We are not only to receive it; we're also called to offer it to others, to live it out on a daily basis, to extend the grace of God in the midst of difficult and trying and sometimes unfair circumstances.

A Brutal World

It was a typical scene in the high school cafeteria: the athletes were sitting together at the "popular table," making comments under their breath about a shy and homely girl seated a few tables away.

The whole school knew her to be a pure, old-fashioned girl, and her traditional values often made her the butt of jokes. On this particular day, the ringleader of the guys said, "I'll bet you fifty dollars I can have that girl skinny-dipping with me in one month!"

His buddies knew he had one of the worst reputations in the school, and they were convinced this girl would never even agree to go out with him. So they said, "Fifty bucks? You're on!"

So the young man went into action. The next day he started saying, "Hi!" to her in the hallway, and then one day he complimented her on the way she looked. The girl couldn't believe that this handsome sports star even knew she existed!

After a while he started calling her on the phone, and pretty soon he asked her out. He treated her with respect and courtesy, and within a couple weeks they were dating regularly. She was becoming a different girl. She felt confident and touched that someone had looked beyond her unattractive veneer to see her inner beauty.

The night before the month was up, the two of them went walking around the school. The young man said, "Hey, you wanna go swimming?"

"Sure," she said, "but where?"

"Well, one of the privileges of being captain of the swim team is having a key to the indoor pool."

"But I don't have a swimsuit here," she said.

He thought for a second and said, "You know what? It will be so dark in there, we won't really be able to see. Let's just go skinny-dipping."

And she agreed.

So they went inside, took off their clothes, and slipped into the water. No sooner did they get into the pool when the guy's friends, who were hiding in the bleachers, flipped on all the lights, illuminating the entire pool.

"You did it!" one of his friends hollered. "I can't believe you actually pulled it off."

"I told you I could," he yelled back. "You owe me fifty bucks!"

The brazen teen got out of the water and looked down at the girl standing in the pool, trying her best to cover her nakedness. "You're not only ugly," he said, "but you're stupid too!" And the guys walked out, celebrating and laughing.

It's a brutal world. A broken, painful, and cruel world. Our human nature wants to strike out, get even, dispense justice. "Retaliation has its appeal," Max Lucado reminds us. "But Jesus has a better idea."[18]

Jesus' idea, of course, is forgiveness. But how do you learn to forgive, rebound, and recover from such intense hurt?

The Extra Mile

In Jesus' day, when the Romans ruled Palestine and held the Jewish people under the heel of their oppression, the laws were clearly designed to benefit the citizens of Rome, and the Jews were required to obey. If a Roman soldier asked for assistance, a Jewish citizen had to drop whatever he was doing and comply. Immediately. Without question or complaint.

We see an example of this law in the Bible, when Simon of Cyrene was singled out of the crowd and commanded to carry Jesus' cross (Luke 23:26). Simon had no option. Failure to obey opened the door to physical abuse or arrest.

The Roman government limited the law so that a soldier could not demand someone to walk more than one mile. Some Jews marked off an exact mile in four directions from their neighborhood so they wouldn't walk *one step* farther than the law required. And that is the law Jesus referred to in the Sermon on the Mount when He wanted to make a point about revenge and retaliation.

Imagine the scene. The crowd is listening intently, nodding in agreement until Jesus makes this controversial statement: "If anyone forces you to go one mile, go with them two miles" (Matthew 5:41).

Suddenly heads begin to shake.

People scowl and mumble.

"Serve the enemy? What's He thinking? No way!" Perhaps few things Jesus ever said upset His audience as much as this statement did.

"A Christian should be willing to do more than is reasonably expected," pastor Bob Russell explains. "Followers of Jesus Christ should be more congenial, more industrious, more generous, more thoughtful than anticipated—even toward those who have authority over us and treat us poorly."[19]

When I was planning these books, I asked a number of families, "What's the toughest lesson to teach to your kids?" The number one response was "loving your enemies." That item would probably top our list as adults too. It's a hard thing to learn—and it's even harder to model.

But as hard as loving our enemies may be, if we want to raise godly, gracious, generous children who reflect the image of Christ, they need to see us live out that principle as we deal with people.

Several times in Romans 12, Paul spoke to the topic of enemies and those who persecute you. He said, "Dear friends, never take revenge. Leave that to the righteous anger of God. . . . Instead, 'If your enemies are hungry, feed them. If they are thirsty, give them something to drink'" (Romans 12:19–20 NLT).

Grace. Unmerited favor. We've received it, and we are to offer it to others.

It's a principle we need to master.

Extra Grace Required

My friend Pastor Chip Ingram describes difficult and draining individuals as EGR—*Extra Grace Required*—people. These are people who genuinely need a touch of grace from God, a touch that can come through us. I'm sure you have EGR children in your life:

- that brash, bullying, selfish kid in your child's playgroup who has received justice, condemnation, and ostracism—but not much mercy
- the sullen, rebellious teen whose father disappeared years ago and whose overworked mother has no energy left for tenderness, laughter, or patience
- the whiny, spoiled brat whose doting parents give her everything but discipline

Even we as grown-ups find such children difficult to deal with. When your kids encounter such a situation, don't expect them to know automatically how to deal with it. Teach them some practical ways to deal with challenging situations:

- Help your child understand possible causes. Ask your child, "Why do you think that kid in your class acts that way or makes fun of your faith? Do you think he wants attention? Is he insecure?" Remember to practice looking *into* people more than *at* people. Help your children understand the possible reasons behind someone's poor choices. Circumstances don't excuse behavior, but understanding what's behind the action may help your child empathize with it.

- Teach your kids to treat everyone the same way. In James 2 we're told not to show partiality or favoritism. Jesus didn't. He honored everyone above Himself. Try to help your children break away from cliques and develop friendships with kids outside their own social circle. If you challenge your kids to be a friend to everyone and treat everyone the same, your child will reap the benefits.

- Involve others. If your child is having difficulty with a particular classmate and can't seem to resolve the issue, make the teacher or a parent aware of what's going on so that person can keep a watchful eye and, if necessary, intercede. Involve other kids too. Maybe a well-adjusted kid in the peer group or an older sibling might help.

- Remove your child from the problem. Sometimes the wisest thing is to remove your child from the setting or the problem child. In Romans 12:18, Paul said, "If it is possible, as far as it depends on you, live at peace with everyone." *If it is possible.* Paul wouldn't have begun with a conditional clause if harmonious relationships were always possible. Your goal is to raise well-adjusted kids who love the Lord—not martyrs. When the situation warrants, teach your children that, in this particular situation, they need not go out of their way to cross paths with this individual who creates conflict.

- Prepare your children. The dinner table is a great place to discuss real-life situations. Share your own "bully stories" and share how you dealt with them. Prepare your kids to go against the crowd—and that looks different in different situations. Sometimes we run with God. Sometimes we walk with God. And then, as we see in Ephesians 6:11 and 14, there are those moments when the best we can do is stand with God. Sometimes we simply have to take a stand and endure ridicule or torment. When those moments arise, remind your child: "We've talked and prayed about this. You are prepared and ready, and you're not alone."

- Regularly *pray* about those "thorns in the flesh." This may be the most important challenge on this list. Bring those EGR people to the Lord. Pray for them. Teach your kids to pray not just for their friends and families, but also for the people who bring difficulty into their lives. It's harder to dislike someone you pray for on a regular basis.

It's harder to dislike someone you pray for on a regular basis.

Prayer changes things.
Usually it changes us.

The Power of Love

When I was in the sixth grade, there was a guy in my class named Brian. He always seemed to have a chip on his shoulder. He also had a penchant for punching me in the arm—quite hard.

But whenever my mom saw Brian, she offered him a ride home from basketball practice. Every car ride was laced with her maternal encouragement, an invitation to church, and a warm reminder that Mom was praying for Brian. And Brian seemed to appreciate it, even though my bruised bicep didn't. But Brian became a friend and, in time, a Christian.

Over thirty years later I was shocked to get a phone call from Brian, whom I hadn't seen since I was twelve. Somehow he had tracked me down, and he wanted my mom's address. He felt prompted to write her.

In the course of the conversation, Brian told me that he believed my mom's prayers and encouragement got him through a tough time. During junior high, his dad was an alcoholic who could be quite abusive. He didn't feel safe riding with his dad, so he would opt to walk if no one offered him a ride.

But my perceptive mom realized that Brian didn't need avoidance; he needed attention. Mom saw what I couldn't see—that a sore arm paled in comparison to the value of my friend seeing a functional family who followed the Lord.

The Best Reason to Forgive

There are lots of good reasons to forgive.

William A. Ward said, "Forgiveness is a funny thing. It warms the heart and cools the sting."[20]

Joyce Meyer says, "The best way to have the last word is to apologize."[21]

Jesus said, "Forgive, and you will be forgiven" (Luke 6:37).

But the most important reason to forgive is that when you do—when you extend grace to others, when you honor those who don't deserve it—you begin to look like Jesus.

The same Jesus who looked down from the cross at the people who had nailed Him there and said, "Father, forgive them; for they know not what they do" (Luke 23:34 KJV). Jesus also said this: "Love your enemies . . . Bless those who curse you" (Luke 6:27–28).

Forgive them, because they need to be forgiven.

Love them, because they need to be loved.

Bless them, because they need to be blessed.

God calls us to "do justice" in the world, to create a world where the weak are protected from the manipulation and cruelty of the strong (Micah 6:8 ESV). God calls us to reflect the image of the Divine in the world, to find creative ways to love and serve others, even those who are unlovable and unappreciative. God calls us to be Christ to others.

God calls us.

He calls you and me.

So reach out. But first reach deep into the undeserved deposits of grace God has so lavishly placed into the storehouse of riches in your own heart. Open up the doors and windows, and give without asking anything in return. Offer grace and compassion not because people deserve it or even because they ask for it, but simply because they need it.

The same way you needed it.

The same way God offered it to you.

Whether you ever see the fruit of your efforts or not, know that the love and grace you offer *will* change people.

It changes us all.

Forever.

8

Pride, Prejudice, and Position

Live in harmony with one another. Do not be proud, but be willing to associate with people of low position. Do not be conceited.

Romans 12:16

D on't do it again!" the big kid on my street threatened.

The year was 1972. I had moved to Missouri in the middle of the school year, and that is a real challenge for a fifth grader. Fortunately I was able to make some friends on the basketball team, and I soon learned that one of them, a guy named Don, lived within a mile of my house. I invited him over to ride bikes—and he did.

Much to my surprise, that invitation caused quite a stir. People whispered.

Eyebrows were raised when I walked to the bus stop the next day.

The bully on our street threatened me with a black eye if I ever did it again.

Cut me some slack! I didn't know any better.

You see, my parents had never taught me not to be friends with somebody who had darker skin or lived in a housing project. Instead, Mom and Dad raised me with the belief that we were all God's children. They taught me about a God who really isn't concerned about the neighborhood we live in or whether we're born with a deep tan or have to spend our summers trying to get one.

My parents taught me that God is much more concerned with what we look like on the inside. God looks deeper.

But when I was eleven, I didn't know any better. Now, forty years later, I hope I still don't. In fact, I pray that color blindness is a trait I've passed on to my kids.

Judge, Jury, and Jesus

As human beings, we're pretty gifted when it comes to sizing others up. If they don't have our level of education or live in a place as nice as ours; if their skin color or language or religious heritage is different; or if they walk funny or talk funny (or can't walk or talk at all), we look down on them. Each one of us has our own litmus test—spoken or unspoken, subtle or overt—by which we measure others against ourselves.

Ever wonder why our schools are populated with little cliques of friends who all look alike? Well, left to their own devices, kids tend to buddy up with peers who are more or less like them. This tendency may be due to insecurity or peer pressure, but whatever the cause, it shows up every single day in the school lunchroom and on the playground.

The truth is, even we adults tend to gravitate to people who are similar to us. Maybe we're insecure. Maybe we're worried about how people around us will perceive us if we associate with a certain person. But if we never step out beyond that comfort zone, if we never get close to folks who are not like us, we miss the opportunity to grow and stretch and learn and share and deepen our emotional and spiritual lives. If your worth is based on other people's opinions of you, you will never break away from your comfortable circle of friends; you will never have your life enriched by people who are different.

Our kids need to experience these same important opportunities for relational and spiritual growth. To help make that happen, consider these questions:

- **How can our children learn to see people for who they are on the inside instead of the outside?**
- **How do we teach them to befriend those who are beyond the borders of their comfortable circles?**

- **What can we parents do to help our kids take an interest in the disabled, the disadvantaged, or the just plain different?**

Like every other spiritual principle, our children learn either prejudice or inclusivity from us. Our kids see how we live, what we value, and the way we treat people. So if you don't like what you see in your children, look in the mirror. The fact is, they often become what you model for them.

So make it your personal goal to live the way Jesus lived. Jesus, who valued all people, who welcomed the outcasts and sinners, who ignored the gossip and the accusations from the Pharisees, and went about the business of loving people the way God loved them.

Routinely ask your kids if they notice anyone in the neighborhood or at school who seems to be overlooked or disconnected from others. Help your children get into the habit of including some of those kids. Their outreach may breathe life into someone who is discouraged, downtrodden, or disconnected. And rather than gaining popularity for themselves, your kids are giving worth—and that's far more important.

Beyond that, teach your children that reaching out to people is not an act of charity; it's simply the way that Christians live. We don't accept others because we're "doing good" for them; we accept them because it's the right thing to do and in enlarging the boundaries of our own lives, we find ourselves more enriched.

Economics: What You Own

I n our adult lives we tend to categorize people according to the prestige of their career, the salary associated with their job, or the neighborhood in which they live. And the sad truth is, we make judgments based on some of the silliest things. One of my wife's friends told a woman at church that she buys hand-me-down clothes at consignment shops. "By the expression on her face," Beth's friend said, "you would have thought I'd announced I pulled castoffs out of the trash in a leper colony."

When the labels on our clothes are more important than the person inside, it's time to step back and reevaluate. But make no mistake: the prejudice associated with material things is a two-way street. If you grew up *without* money, you might have been raised to think that everyone who is wealthy is stingy, arrogant, and self-centered. If you were raised *with* money, you may be tempted to measure the worth of people based on their financial portfolio rather than on the fact that God created them in His image. The Bible warns us that prejudice in this particular area can go in both directions: "Do not show partiality to the poor or favoritism to the great, but judge your neighbor fairly" (Leviticus 19:15).

The majority of us are somewhere in the middle of these two extremes, so our prayer can be: "Give me neither poverty nor riches, but give me only my daily bread" (Proverbs 30:8).

Contentment. It's a radical concept.

It's also God's way.

Race: How You Look

Years ago, in the early 1900s, a wealthy family in the Deep South was known for sharing food with African Americans who were desperately trying to make ends meet. One day a black man came to the front door of the family's mansion. When the woman of the house answered, he awkwardly asked if she had any food she could share with him. She warily glanced in all directions and whispered, "Go around and meet me at the back door."

There she gave him a bag of bread, but before he could take a bite, she said, "I want you to repeat after me the Lord's Prayer: 'Our Father who art in heaven.'"

The man said, "*Your* Father who art in heaven."

She corrected him. "No. Repeat after me: *our* Father."

Again he said, "*Your* Father who art in heaven."

She was perturbed and said, "Why do you keep saying *Your Father*?"

"Ma'am," the black man responded, "if I said, *Our Father*, that would mean that you and I were brother and sister. If we truly were brother and sister, then you wouldn't have made me come around to your back porch."[22]

Sometimes we do good things, but we stop short of doing the best things.

My parents knew that you never change the mind-set of others by cowering to intimidation and the ignorance of bullies on your street. Despite raised eyebrows, whispered comments, or even the threat of a black eye, my friend Don came to my house again and again. I'd have missed out on a great friendship if Mom and Dad hadn't raised me to focus on character more than accents, skin color, or designer labels.

When the prophet Samuel went to the home of Jesse to anoint a new king for Israel, he looked down the ranks of Jesse's sons—strong, handsome, courageous warriors—and thought, *Surely one of these guys must be the one.*

But God told Samuel that none of them would do. God's choice for the role was David, the scrawny little brother, the skinny kid who spent all his time out in the fields with the sheep teaching himself how to play a harp and shoot a slingshot. When Samuel questioned God, wanting to make sure he had the right brother, God told him, "People look at the outward appearance, but the LORD looks at the heart" (1 Samuel 16:7).

Look beyond appearances. Value the heart.

It's God's way.

Status: Where You Live

Salli was driving her three young boys when she pulled off the interstate exit. A homeless man approached their car, and the kids didn't understand why their mom didn't give him anything. Salli explained the reality that money given like that often gets spent on bad things. Then one of her sons asked, "But what if he really is in need?"

Well, Salli didn't have a great answer for him, but to her credit she didn't just blow off his question. Instead, Salli and her husband Josh, along with their kids, started a ministry to the homeless in that area, and they invited other families to get involved in serving these forgotten people.

Now, a year later, fifty different families have volunteered at one time or another. They feed the homeless on a weekly basis. Their kids encourage and play games with small children who at times must stay in a short-term home in the area. Their young children pray by name for the hurting people they've met. And they all learned that homeless people are just like everybody else: whatever their problems, they just want someone to show them a measure of love.

It takes some effort, some intentionality, to rid ourselves of the hidden veins of prejudice in our lives and begin to embrace everyone around us with the love of Christ. But it's critical to face our unfounded fears and to model for our children and teach them by precept that God loves all of us.

Chip Ingram says, "Subtle as it may be, when you make a decision about the value or significance of a person you don't know for whatever external reason, the Bible calls it prejudice, and it is a big deal to God."[23]

God is consumed with the heart and the motives, not with stuff or status or similarities. And when He looks at differences, He sees potential instead of problems. If we raise our kids to "look good" and impress others, we aren't imitating God; we're conforming to the world around us. But when we see people the way God sees them, we look at everyone from a totally different perspective. In Matthew 25, Jesus shed a new light on the matters of equality, inclusivity, and acceptance:

> I was hungry and you gave me something to eat, I was thirsty and you gave me something to drink, I was a stranger and you invited me in, I needed clothes and you clothed me, I was sick and you looked after me, I was in prison and you came to visit me.... Truly I tell you, whatever you did for one of the least of these brothers and sisters of mine, you did for me. (Matthew 25:35–36, 40)

Realizing that everyone we encounter is Jesus in disguise makes an enormous difference in our perspective. Jesus wearing designer jeans or hand-me-down dungarees. Jesus living in a palace or a cardboard box under a bridge. Jesus dawning a turban or sporting a shaved head. Jesus covered with black skin, brown skin, white skin.

We should treat everyone the way we would treat Jesus.

So affirm your children when you see that behavior in them. And when they miss an opportunity, try to discover why they held back. In time, acceptance can become second nature for them, a healthy habit that puts a smile on God's face.

After all, Jesus interacted with people at every level of the social strata. He honored women. He welcomed the very young and the very old. He encouraged the poor. He had close friends who were wealthy and close friends who were homeless. He dined with prostitutes. He interacted with religious leaders. He did lunch with the most despised in society.

Clearly, Jesus didn't show favoritism to any class or group. Neither should we. When your kids see that Christlike spirit in you, they will be more apt to treat everyone with honor. They will also begin to bear an uncanny resemblance to their Lord.

When we see people the way God sees them, we look at everyone from a totally different perspective.

The Difference Is *You*

My Uncle Greg, who died several years ago, had cerebral palsy. He was a quadriplegic, only able to get around with an electric wheelchair. His speech was quite difficult to understand, and although this struggle to communicate must have been frustrating for him, he was always patient with our poor efforts to decipher the simplest phrase.

Back in the late 1990s, Greg attended a weeklong church camp designed for those who were developmentally disabled. One of the volunteers at that camp was a nineteen-year-old church member named John Miller.

These were uncharted waters for John. Yet when he was assigned to my Uncle Greg, John devoted himself to the caregiving tasks twenty-four hours a day for four days. He helped Greg in and out of his wheelchair. He fed him every bite and gave him every drink. He helped Greg bathe and even assisted him in the bathroom. John did everything for Greg.

One day John and three other guys took Greg down to the lake. They helped him get into a special flotation device, and for the first time in his life Greg went swimming. It was quite an experience.

The closing ceremony was an extraordinary time for these special campers. First the counselors and volunteers said some things about the new friends they had assisted at camp. Then the campers shared what the highlight of the week was for them. Almost all of them said the same thing—swimming!

When it was Greg's turn, John shared with everyone all about my Uncle Greg. He told how much Greg loved the water and that they had nicknamed him "the Fish."

Then John asked Greg the big question: "What was your favorite thing at camp?"

Although Greg is often hard to understand, there was no mistaking what happened next. My uncle awkwardly raised his arm, pointed his finger at John, and said, "You!"

Caught off guard, John said, "Well, Greg, there had to be something else. Was it the swimming? Or the snack time?"

But once again Greg lifted his shaky hand and said, "You!"

John's life and Uncle Greg's life were vastly different, yet between them a friendship had formed. That tends to happen when people genuinely value one another.

Through his gratitude Greg gave John value.

Through his service John gave Greg value.

Not a bad trade.

Lifting Others Up

Let love be genuine.

ROMANS 12:9 ESV

Before we leave, I need to thank that man," said six-year-old Ella. Her babysitter assumed the man was a family friend. So before exiting the restaurant, the young girl headed over to the man wearing his army fatigues and eating a taco.

"Hi," she said. "My name is Ela. Thank you for fighting for our country."

That was all. No prodding, no instruction. All on her own, a six-year-old girl took the initiative to encourage a stranger.

The soldier could hardly believe it. The babysitter could hardly believe it! She watched while her small charge and the burly soldier engaged in a brief conversation. Then Ela turned and was ready to leave. Her business was finished.

How does that happen? How does a six-year-old know to show honor to a stranger?

Does it just happen?

No, it happens because Jason and Daniela consistently teach their young daughter to be on the lookout for people she can honor. Ela is eager to lift the spirits of others—whether or not her parents are present.

Crabs and Cheerleaders

Years ago a friend told me that if you catch several crabs and place them in a basket, you won't need a lid.

"Won't they just crawl up and out?" I asked.

"No," he said. "If one of them starts its ascent and rises to the top, the others will pull him back down."

Modern society is a study in crab behavior. We're swimming in a sea of sarcasm. We gossip and talk back and criticize and spew out negativity. We undermine our enemies—and even our friends—without thinking twice about it. From the playground to the boardroom, tearing others down has become commonplace.

If you don't think so, just look around you. Whenever anyone gets too much praise or attention, some crabby person will feel it's time to bring the person back down. Kids who discourage other kids and run them down typically belong to parents who specialize in belittling. They are parroting their parents.

But that's not the way Jesus lived.

Jesus was a cheerleader, a congratulator, an encourager—and for some of the most unexpected people too. He went around touching lepers, welcoming prostitutes, forgiving adulterers. He even went to dinner with a hated tax collector named Zacchaeus when the so-called "holy people" of Jericho wouldn't give him the time of day. And Zacchaeus changed his ways on the spot, paid back four times what he had gained by cheating people, and became a follower of the Rabbi who accepted him as he was (Luke 19:1–9).

Encouragement breathes life into people. It gives them a second chance.

Jesus knew the truth: you never make yourself look big by making others look small.

Demolition and Construction

Years ago I was watching the national news with my kids. They showed a clip of Cincinnati's Riverfront Stadium being demolished to make room for a new ballpark. We watched this huge structure tumble to the ground in a matter of eleven seconds.

I grew up in Cincinnati, so I was able to tell my kids about the excitement in the city back when I was eight years old and the construction began. It had taken two years to build the massive stadium. My children were fascinated as I recalled watching the slow construction process unfold.

And then of course I seized this teachable moment! "Anyone can tear others down," I said, "but it takes effort and intentionality to build people up. You can say all kinds of encouraging words to someone," I told them. "But in a matter of seconds you can tear apart months of friendship with one cruel or hate-filled remark."

In the weeks to come, whenever I overheard a discouraging or negative comment coming from one of my kids, I'd ask, "Are you going to be in the construction business or the demolition business?"

The apostle Paul called us to "encourage one another and build each other up" (1 Thessalonians 5:11). We need to be proactive: we need to look for ways to challenge our children to lift someone up—consistently and frequently.

Most of us would say we're not into tearing people down. But how often do we remain uninvolved instead of going out of our way to say or do something positive? Do we let ourselves off the hook, assuming that others will take on the mantle of encouragement?

Yet in the absence of encouragement, discouragement prevails. If we're not building up, we're tearing down . . . by default.

A house left alone will crumble to the ground.

On the Lookout

When our kids were younger and our family would pull up to school or to someone's home, Beth or I would say, "Let's have our antennae up!" This was code language for "Look for ways God can use you to encourage someone." Planting seeds in your children's minds gives them an awareness of the role they can play in honoring others. Sowing that thought can be as simple as stating an age-appropriate expectation:

- **"When we go inside, have some questions ready for Mr. or Mrs. Clements. We want to take an interest in them tonight."**
- **"If someone is sitting alone in the school cafeteria today, invite her to join you and your friends."**
- **"When you arrive at a line or a door at the same time as someone else, smile and allow that person to go ahead of you."**
- **"If someone is being made fun of, say something positive about the individual or attempt to change the direction of the conversation."**

Evidence is everywhere that we need encouragement to encourage others . . .

Recently my wife was mulching in the front yard. Some kids walked past and said, "Hi, Mrs. Stone!" They talked with her for a minute or two before heading off to fish at a nearby pond.

A few minutes later a fourteen-year-old straggler named Cade came by. "Hi, Mrs. Stone," he said. "Would you like me to help you with your mulching?"

Beth said, "Wow, that is really nice of you, Cade, but I'm almost finished. Thanks for offering to help." And he went on to catch up with the others.

You may think such adolescent servanthood would never happen in your neighborhood. You may believe you are the only faithful family around your apartment complex or subdivision. And you may be right . . . but your community doesn't need to stay that way.

You can change your environment as your encouragement has a ripple effect on other families and homes. God may have placed you where you are for just this reason. As you grow in this discipline of honoring others, they in turn will pass it on.

In *Building Family Ties with Faith, Love & Laughter*, I discuss an effective teaching method for kids called *Good, Better, Best*. It both applauds and stretches them in their behavior. In the mulch scenario:

- *Good* would be to say, "Hello" to my wife as they walked by.
- *Better* is the group stopping and talking with Beth.
- *Best* was Cade's extra-mile effort to stop, talk, *and* volunteer to serve her. Cade's sincere offer took honor to another level.

Anonymous Encouragers

It was a summer day, and thirteen-year-old Trevor was enjoying doing nothing. He was sitting in front of the television passing the time when his father said, "I was just talking to Mrs. Brown as she was heading to the grocery. I wonder if you could secretly mow her lawn before she returns."

The concept captured Trevor's curiosity. His father continued, "Twenty years from now you'll never remember what you watched on TV today, but you'll never forget anonymously encouraging your neighbor."

That statement resonated with Trevor, and he sprang into action. He mowed the lawn and blew the excess grass from her driveway. Then he rushed inside and watched stealthily out the window for her return. When Mrs. Brown pulled in, she got out of the car and stood there staring at her yard, baffled, looking in different directions around the neighborhood.

Trevor never divulged what he'd done, and his father's words proved true. To this day he doesn't remember anything about the television shows he watched that day. But decades later, he's never forgotten how he felt when his intentional and secret act of kindness encouraged a neighbor in need.

Encouraging Words

The most encouraging kids are those whose parents feed them a steady diet of genuine encouragement. Not an endless barrage of sappy and syrupy words, but genuine, honest words of affirmation. There's a simple explanation for why that parental habit continues with their children. When our words lift up our kids and resonate with them, they will want to repeat that same process so that others can, in turn, feel joy and security.

So spend time encouraging your children. Pay attention. Catch them doing something good and affirm them. Your investment will pay huge dividends in their individual lives, future family relationships, and self-confidence. Not convinced? Here's a story for you.

Bob Feller was a tremendous major league pitcher who received the highest honor by being inducted into the Hall of Fame. He'd had all-star game invitations, thrown

Spend time encouraging your children. Pay attention. Catch them doing something good and affirm them.

no-hitters, and even played in the World Series. You name it—he accomplished it on the baseball field.

Years after his career was over, Feller was asked, "If you could go back and relive any baseball memory from your life, what would it be?"

Feller thought for a minute and then answered, "I would like to return to playing catch with my father."[24]

Amazing. From among the most exciting moments possible in baseball, played in front of thousands, even millions, of fans, Bob Feller opted for tossing the ball in his backyard with his dad.

Perhaps that gives us some insight into the encouraging words he heard, words that undoubtedly propelled him to become an exceptional player.

God's Helpers

Recently my teenage nephew Justin was attending a church camp in Ohio. The forecast called for a week of record heat with no end in sight. On the first day he made a lot of new friends, including Rob, a brand-new camper in his cabin. Rob was obviously unfamiliar with the kind of clothes to bring, and he was sweating and miserable in jeans and a heavy shirt.

So Justin called his mom to see if she could buy a couple of pairs of shorts and some tank tops and bring them to the camp. The next day Justin secretly put the new clothes in Rob's sleeping bag with this note: *This is from God's helpers.* When Rob found the note and the clothes, he was elated.

None of the other campers knew about it. Rob was able to keep his dignity without looking like a charity project. By not making a spectacle—by meeting the need anonymously—Justin and his mom greatly encouraged this rookie camper.

Encouragement is a lot like giving: it blesses both the one who is encouraged and the encourager. Give your kids opportunities to experience the joy and the blessing that come when they willingly become God's (sometimes anonymous) helpers.

Such encouragement may come quite naturally for some of your kids, but it may feel foreign to others. Either way, keep at it: show them how to be on the lookout for people to encourage. In time, your children will realize that a simple word or thoughtful deed can transform someone's day.

It might even change someone's life.

The Simplest Way

One of the most encouraging gifts we can give doesn't cost a penny, nor does it involve effort, sweat, or any inconvenience. In fact, it involves saying just one word—a person's name.

Think about it. The sweetest sound on earth is hearing your little baby say "Ma-Ma" or "Da-Da." Hearing your beloved call you "sweetheart." Hearing a new acquaintance or friend speak your name. When someone knows your name, it shows that you are important; it communicates that you have value. Someone has taken the time to look past the surface and remember who you are.

On the other hand, when somebody gets your name wrong, you feel deflated, undervalued, even invisible.

Names matter.

Last year my two younger kids accompanied my wife and me on a cruise where I was speaking. About one-third of the ship's 1500 passengers was involved in the Christian programming we offered. I challenged Sam and Sadie each to learn the names of one hundred people they didn't know. They made a competition of it. When the cruise was over, we spent the next hour in the car listening to them rattle off the names. Both succeeded, which may explain why both were so loved by the people on board. They got out of their comfort zone. Most impressive was Sam's ability to be on a first-name basis with thirty-five employees and other guests who weren't with our "Christian" group.

He cared enough to get to know them. And it meant something to those individuals.

In *Walking on Water*, Madeleine L'Engle says: "To be given a name is an act of intimacy as powerful as any act of love. . . . To name is to love. To be named is to be loved."[25]

So don't rationalize in front of your kids your failure to learn and remember names. Don't say, "Oh, I'm terrible with names" and let that be your excuse for not encouraging someone by name. When you and your children work at remembering names, you are teaching them to give value to the individuals whose names they learn.

The simple gift of naming communicates that you care.

Lift Them Up

The Navigators Ministry, founded in 1933, is one of the world's most respected faith-based organizations today. The ministry excels in teaching discipleship and encouraging Scripture memory. But perhaps the Navs' greatest service is the ministry of encouragement.

Dawson Trotman, the organization's founder and president, was an encourager who was always focused on others. Always. He lived out the example of Jesus—walking through life with people, meeting them where they were, accepting them, and helping them grow. Not only was he a leader, but he was also a friend to all he met.

One summer day Dawson Trotman spent the afternoon with some adults and kids out on Schroon Lake in New York. Toward the end of the day, Trotman was exhausted from waterskiing much longer than a fifty-year-old probably should have. He climbed back into the boat, and they headed for the dock. Along the way he learned that one of the girls, Allene Beck, couldn't swim. Trotman traded places with her so she would be in a safer spot aboard the boat.

Then the unthinkable happened. The speeding boat encountered a sizable wave that sent both Trotman and Allene flying into the water.

Already fatigued, Dawson Trotman gathered his senses and located Allene, who was thrashing and sinking nearby. He plunged underwater, found her, and brought her to the surface. He fought to keep her head above water.

It took an unusually long time for the boat to get turned around and headed back to where they were. All the while Trotman, exhausted but determined, kept lifting her up so she could breathe. Finally the boat eased up to them, and the others pulled her to safety.

Time Magazine describes what happened next: "But as hands reached down to seize Trotman's hand, he sank out of sight. So died Dawson Trotman."[26]

Can you imagine a sadder story than that? Yet even in his passing, Trotman was doing what he had always done, being who he had always been. He was a selfless man in a self-centered world, focusing on others instead of himself.

Allene Beck, now in her sixties, is living proof of that.

When you are exhausted and don't especially feel like encouraging others, remember Dawson Trotman. He died as he lived: lifting others up.

Just as Ela did for her soldier.

Just as Jesus did for you and me.

May the same be said of you and of your children.

10

Redirecting Your Focus

*Do not conform to the pattern of this world, but
be transformed by the renewing of your mind.*

ROMANS 12:2

Somebody in the Bramer household was paying attention.

A few months ago they read *Raising Your Kids to Love the Lord*, and they learned about our Stone family tradition of saving money to use to encourage individuals throughout our family vacation.

So they put aside the money, stashed it in an envelope, and took it with them. The plan was to encourage a different person each day of their vacation.

One hot day at a swimming pool, the kids went to get a cold drink. They overheard the lady at the concession stand trying to teach her young customers some manners. When it was their turn to order, both Dakota (age eight) and Trinity (age six) spent some time getting to know this woman.

When the Bramer children returned, they told their Mom about Miss Lela, how she was training and encouraging the kids who came up to her. Dakota and Trinity decided they wanted to bless Miss Lela.

They went back to their room and got their special envelope with the money inside. They wrote out a thank-you card, along with a Scripture verse, and they all signed it. Then Dakota and Trinity took it to Miss Lela and explained their daily vacation ritual of choosing someone to bless each day.

One of the kids asked if they could pray about anything for her. She shared some specific requests for her own children. The Bramers then gave her the envelope, and before she even opened it, she began to cry. After opening it and reading the note, she cried some more and gave each of them a hug. She called the Bramers her "angels."

Later that evening, Shannon Bramer emailed me and summed up her thoughts:

> *Wow!* What an amazing experience! We felt more blessed than I believe she did. The greatest part was to watch my girls see how much it meant to the woman. Her tears of joy showed them how

much more blessed it is to give than to receive. These daily experiences have changed the focus of our vacation, and we can't wait to see who God will lead us to bless tomorrow.

Shannon found out what you can discover too: once you start honoring others, you and your kids will find that it's hard to stop. But the key for most all families is to change their focus. To swim against the current, to be counter-cultural.

Tim Kimmel says this about the responsibility we have as parents:

> Even with the disappointments . . . raising children is still the greatest thing you'll ever do. It's greater than any milestone you can hit in your career. It dwarfs any fame you may receive for your ideas or your inventions. You've been handed a piece of history in advance—a gracious gift you send to a time you will not see—and you play the biggest role in how that history will ultimately be recorded.[27]

I'm pleased you read this book.
I'll be more pleased if you put the principles into action.

Reminders for the Journey

T he world doesn't often promote the idea that we should focus on others and transfer the spotlight from our wants to others' needs. So let me remind you that it's still possible in this self-centered world to raise kids who are selfless and think of others.

It's possible. But it is difficult. Really difficult.

It's hard to teach selflessness when we parents struggle with selfishness and greed ourselves—daily. (Guilty.) Life is busy, and it's easy to get caught up doing your own thing. It's easier to let training your child take a backseat to your career, your hobbies, or your relationships. But as we mature spiritually and allow the Holy Spirit to help our self-focus to fade, others receive more of our attention and love. Beth and I have made plenty of mistakes; we aren't perfect parents. We do the best we can and are thankful for God's grace. And we continue to ask for His strength and wisdom . . . just as you do.

Raise Them to Release Them

The psalmist gives us an interesting metaphor for child rearing: "Like arrows in the hands of a warrior are children born in one's youth. Blessed is the man whose quiver is full of them" (Psalm 127:4–5).

An arrow won't get anywhere if you don't let it go. And if an arrow is not released, it can never fulfill its purpose.

What's all this talk about bows and arrows and quivers? Well, for an arrow to serve its purpose, it must be straightened, sharpened, aimed, and finally released.

I repeat: *released*.

An arrow won't get anywhere if you don't let it go. And if an arrow is not released, it can never fulfill its purpose.

Whether we realize it or not, we began releasing our children on day one. Even those first baby steps take them away from us. Their next steps take them farther as they begin to move out on their own: the first day of school, the first sleepover, the first time at camp. Driving, dating, college, marriage—every step of their journey leads them away from the nest into the joys and challenges of their own independent lives.

Now, I'm not getting all syrupy and emotional. After all, I was a student pastor for a number of years, so these truths bring back a flood of memories. When we loaded a bus for middle school camp, the parents would stand on the sidewalk and say, "Be careful. Write me. I'm going to miss you!"

Then, as soon as the bus pulled out, those junior high kids shouted, "We're free! We're free!"

What the kids didn't know was that as soon as the bus pulled out of the parking lot, the *parents* were also shouting, "We're free! We're free!"

Releasing our arrows is a slow and steady process. Over the years we gradually prepare them, teaching them how to love God and treat others with kindness and respect. If we've trained them to honor others above themselves, they glide and soar through life—even life's storms—after we've let go.

Don't get me wrong. There'll be a lump in your throat the size of Texas when you pull away from that college campus. When you move them into that first apartment, you'll discover allergies you never knew you had, invisible pollens that will make your eyes water profusely!

But remember: you are raising your kids to release them.

"It's Too Late for Our Kids"

Okay, so you haven't made all the right decisions. You haven't been consistent with boundaries and conse-quences. You haven't modeled a generous, self-giving, Christlike attitude for your kids. (Join the club! A lot of parents throughout all of time are members!)

Is it ever too late? You may feel that way—but it's not. Connect with your teenager. Reestablish boundaries. Talk to them. Let them see that you're willing to change. Give them something better to aim at.

Recommit yourself to the principles of honoring oth-ers, imitating Christ, and extending grace, forgiveness, and hospitality to those around you. Your example can be a springboard for your children.

The goal is not for people to think you are nice or that your kids are nice. The goal is not to present an image or facade of Christlikeness. The goal is a lifestyle of selfless-ness and a compassionate focus on others, so that people will see Jesus in you and be drawn to Him.

One of the main reasons Jesus came to earth was to be an example of servanthood. "For even the Son of Man," He said, "did not come to be served, but to serve" (Mark 10:45).

The only person in history who could have had a Messiah complex didn't. Jesus knew His visit to this planet wasn't about Him, so He put the spotlight on everyone else.

It's never too late to change.

Coming Full Circle

Years ago our family was eating dinner together when our middle child, Sadie, who was nine at the time, asked, "Hey, Dad, if I reply back to an e-mail from AOL, does some-body read it?"

I said, "Well, yes, if they sent you something, they will have someone read your response."

Our meal continued, and nothing more was said about the e-mail. But Beth and I exchanged an uneasy glance. We both felt unsettled about Sadie's online correspondence with a stranger, and we were quite curious about what she had said to the mystery individual via AOL.

When Sadie left the table, I pulled aside my older daughter, Savannah. "Can you find and print off for me what Sadie received and what she sent to AOL?"

My tech savvy daughter said, "No problem."

A few minutes later Savannah came back with a print-out and said, "It was just a form letter explaining AOL's various services. But you may want to see what Sadie wrote back."

She handed us the reply her sister had sent:

Dear AOL,

Do you know Jesus Christ? Is he your savior? He died on the cross for you and then he arose from the dead! Please axept him as your savior! If you believe in him you will be saved and you don't wan't to go to hell with satin. If you wan't him to be your savior go to the church and be baptized in to Jesus Christ your Lord! You pray to god & ask him to forgive your sins! I hope fully see you in heaven one day!

sadie stone

Not exactly what we were expecting. (Understatement of the year.)

Beth and I were speechless. Evidently some of those early seeds we'd planted had grown. She might not have been the greatest speller, but her heart beat for others—even for total strangers.

In fact, it still does.

What It's All About

Parenting is a tough job and a huge responsibility. But now and then the Lord gives you glimpses inside your child's heart and allows you to see at least a little something of the fruit of your labor. Those moments encourage you to stay the course, to live out the truth of God's Word, and to follow the example of Jesus. And maybe, if you're blessed, you'll see that same child at age twenty-one, her priorities unchanged, still passionate about sharing Christ boldly with others.

"Let's not allow ourselves to get fatigued doing good. At the right time we will harvest a good crop if we don't give up, or quit" (Galatians 6:9 MSG).

Teaching your children to be focused on others takes a lot of focus of your own. It takes intentionality. It takes authenticity. It takes repetition. It takes prayer.

Lots and lots of prayer.

But it's worth it.

I still have a hard copy of Sadie's e-mail reply to AOL. Sometimes I get it out and read it again. It serves as a slap-in-the-face reminder of how I should be spending my time on this earth. It shows me, when I forget, what my life is to be all about:

> **It's about giving rather than getting.**
> **It's about playing second fiddle and letting your light shine.**

It's about opening your hands and your heart and
your home.

It's about extending radical grace to people who don't
deserve it and lifting others up even when it costs you.

It's about others. Life on earth is not just about you.

It's not just about now; it's about eternity.

It's a process. It's a journey. And it's never too late to get
on the road.

Endnotes

1. Steve Rivera, "Emmons loses gold medal after aiming at wrong target," Gannett News Service, August 22, 2004, http://www.usatoday.com/sports/olympics/athens/skill/2004-08-22-shooting-emmons_x.htm.

2. Craig Groeschel on Catalyst podcast, January 17, 2011.

3. Richard D. Dobbins, *Invisible Imprint: What Others Feel When in Your Presence* (Camp Sherman, OR: VMI Publishers, 2002), 87.

4. Quoted in Russ Lawson, "Playing Second Fiddle?" *Heartlight*, September 29, 2009, http://www.heartlight.org/articles/200909/20090929_secondfiddle.html.

5. Ibid.

6. The Etiquette Factory, *Etiquette Intermediate,* accessed September 3, 2012, https://www.theetiquettefactory.com/intermediate.php.

7. Richard Foster, *Celebration of Discipline: The Path to Spiritual Growth* (San Francisco: Harper & Row, 1978), 113–114.

8. Rick Warren, *The Purpose-Driven Life: What on Earth Am I Here For?* (Grand Rapids: Zondervan, 2002), 17.

9. Thanks to Joyce Sharp and Sara Chay for their help on this section.

10. Gary and Anne Marie Ezzo, *Growing Kids God's Way*, 5th ed. (Simi Valley, CA: Biblical Ethics for Parenting, 1999), 135.

11. Tim Tebow with Nathan Whitaker, Through My Eyes (New York: Harper Collins, 2011), 14.

12. Quoted in Tryon Edwards, ed., *A Dictionary* t*of Thoughts: Being a Cyclopedia of Laconic Quotations from the Best Authors of the World, Both Ancient and Modern* (Detroit, MI: F. B. Dickerson Company, 1908), 515.

13. Warren Wiersbe, *Be Wise: Discern the Difference Between Man's Knowledge and God's Wisdom*, 2nd ed. (Colorado Springs, CO: David C. Cook, 2010), 177.

14. Quoted in Dudley Rutherford, *God Has an App for That!: Discover God's Solutions for the Major Issues of Life* (Ventura, CA: Regal, 2012), 7.

15. Greek: 'cheerful' ἱλαρός *hilaros,* accessed June 26, 2012 from Greattreasures.org.

16. Elizabeth Asquith Bibesco, accessed September 3, 2012, http://www.quotationspage.com/quote/31008.html.

17. Cal Thomas, "The Greatest of These Is Love" (sermon, Southeast Christian Church, Louisville, KY, July 21, 1991).

18. Max Lucado, *Grace: More Than We Deserve, Greater Than We Imagine* (Nashville, TN: Thomas Nelson, 2012), 56.

19. Bob Russell, "Going the Extra Mile" (sermon, Southeast Christian Church, Louisville, KY, August 28, 2005).

20. William Arthur Ward, accessed September 3, 2012, http://www.finestquotes.com/author_quotes-author-William%20Arthur%20Ward-page-0.htm.

21. Quoted in Pamela Jason, *101 Church Signs: God's Best Ad Men* (Bloomington, IN: iUniverse, 2010), 27.

22. Adapted from James W. English, Handyman of the Lord: The Life and Ministry of the Reverend William Holmes Borders (New York: Meredith Press, 1967), 33–34.

23. Chip Ingram, "Why We Wound Others with Our Words, Part 2," *Five Lies That Ruin Relationships* (Atlanta, GA: Living on the Edge, 2008), DVD.

24. Told to Bob Russell by a member of the management team of the Baseball Hall of Fame, Cooperstown, New York, June 18.

25. Madeleine L'Engle, *Walking on Water: Reflections on Faith and Art* (Wheaton, IL: Harold Shaw, 1980), 127, 130.

26. "Religion: The Navigator," *Time*, July 2, 1956, http://www.time.com/time/magazine/article/0,9171,891299,00.html.

27. Tim Kimmel, *Grace-Based Parenting* (Nashville: Thomas Nelson, 2004), 2.

Also from Dave Stone

Please share how *How to Raise Selfless Kids in a Self-Centered World* has impacted your family: